JENNIE'S STORY &
UNDER THE SKIN

BETTY LAMBERT

Playwrights Canada Press
Toronto

Playwrights Canada Press
54 Wolseley St., 2nd fl. Toronto, Ontario CANADA M5T 1A5
Tel: (416) 703-0201 Fax: (416) 703-0059
e-mail: orders@puc.ca   http://www.puc.ca

Playwrights Canada Press acknowledges the support of The Canada Council for the Arts for our publishing programme
and the Ontario Arts Council.

Cover photo: William Mockridge, Clare Coulter and Nora McLellan in the 1983 Centre Stage production of 'Jennie's Story." Photo by Robert C. Ragsdale. Playwright photo byGlen E. Erikson.

Canadian Cataloguing in Publication Data
Lambert, Betty, 1933-1983
      Two plays
Contents: Jennie's Story - Under the skin
ISBN 0-88754-462-2
1. Title.
PS8573.A385A6 1987   C812'.54   C87-095158-0
PR9199.3.1.285A6 1987
First edition: November 1987. Second printing: September, 1990. Third printing: July 1997: Fourth printing January 2002.
Printed and bound in Winnipeg, Manitoba. Canada - Hignell Printing.

CONTENTS

INTRODUCTION

Betty Lambert died in 1983. She was at the height of her powers as a playwright, and if she had lived would have, I'm quite sure, continued to write powerful mature works for the stage.

Her association with me, and the New Play Centre, began in the summer and fall of 1973. She gave me the first draft of the first scene of what was to become *Sqrieux-de-Dieu*. She gave it to me to consider for a production of short works named "Collage I and II" which we were presenting at the Arts Club Theatre, on Seymour Street. That program contained a number of pieces by writers who were to become longtime associates, but none more productively than Betty.

Sqrieux-de-Dieu, in its final two-act form, was produced by the New Play Centre in August, 1975. It was a big commercial hit by Vancouver standards in those days, and really marked the beginning of the final phase of Betty's writing for the adult theatre. She had written a number of successful plays for children, and of course was well known as an award-winning radio writer, but up to 1975 her stage efforts for adults had been fairly sporadic. The Playhouse Second Stage had produced *The Visitor*, directed by Joy Coghill, in the fall of 1968, but the script had not ventured beyond the initial exposure. *Sqrieux-de-Dieu*, on the other hand, was an instant success, and went on to further productions in eastern Canada.

Richard Ouzounian, the first director of *Sqrieux-de-Dieu*, while Artistic Director of Festival Lennoxville, approached me to co-commission a work from Betty. The play that finally emerged was the flawed *Clouds of Glory*. Initially seen in our co-production at the Vancouver East Cultural Centre in the spring of 1979, and later that season at Lennoxville, the play proved simultaneously too obscure in theme and too obvious in general plot and characterization to be successful with audiences and critics alike. The concept, an allegory of the October Crisis as seen through the political machinations on a western university campus, was challenging, and funny, but the final draft, and the production, were both unsatisfactory.

In late 1979 I commissioned three plays by local writers. Betty was one of the writers, and we began to discuss and work on a play concerning the backstage life of a "dresser." The idea was based on Betty's experience with a longtime dresser at one of the Vancouver theatres, and a number of scenes had been written when two things happened: the British play, *The Dresser*, became generally known; and, Betty's energies with the idea began to flag. We agreed to put it in the bottom drawer and begin again. What finally emerged—in retrospect, a flash of creativity—was *Jennie's Story*. We did some work on the early draft, a workshop or two, and Betty did some rewriting, but the play as finally produced was very close to its original draft. This process, if it can be called that, was indicative, I believe, of Betty's talent: an intense, emotional connection to the material that poured out; but oddly, for so intellectual a woman, an inability to do, or perhaps a real dislike for the process of, rewriting.

The original New Play Centre production, directed by Jace van der Veen, was first seen at a Canadian Theatre Conference, in Saskatoon. The same production then played at the Waterfront Theatre in Vancouver, to good response, in the fall of 1981. It has since been produced a number of times, and each production has brought forth an audience response commensurate with the emotional intensity of the play; a response to the levels of truth in the anger, joy, love and hate that it expresses. The fundamental strength of the play is that it evokes terror and compassion.

Betty's last work was again initiated by discussions we had—primarily over the phone, for by now Betty was not well—about her writing a play for the New Play Centre. By the time her draft of *Under the Skin* arrived on my desk, we knew that she was dying of cancer, and that she probably had little time left for work. We did discuss the play again, over the phone and through letters, and again through the mail with Bill Glassco who had, since his Toronto production of *Jennie's Story*, been a great favourite of Betty's. We had hoped to gather a workshop in the summer of 1983, but Betty never recovered sufficiently to work on the play seriously. I held that draft of the play for some 18 months before finally deciding to produce it, in the fall of 1985. Of the four Lambert scripts produced by the New Play Centre, *Under the Skin* was the only one that I was to direct. The first production, beautifully acted by the cast, was one of the most intense and theatrically enriching rehearsal periods of my life. The play refused to let go of us, and we lived it day and night, up through the opening. We played the script as written, with only a very few minor cuts taken during rehearsal. The script printed here is our production draft.

The play is based on an actual event, which took place in a suburb of Vancouver. Betty had read the newspaper accounts, and the horror of the story had remained with her. That the play, given its basis, and written at a time in the author's own life when she was forced to deal with her own rapidly declining health, should also embody a message about the ultimate toughness of the human spirit, is to me inspiring. The initial audiences who saw the play in Vancouver (played without intermission) all spoke of the unyielding intensity of the dread of the experience and yet, at the same time, the affirmation of human life that the play contains.

My relationship with Betty, and the very productive relationship of Betty and the New Play Centre, was important personally, and professionally. It is indeed unfortunate that she did not live to continue writing for the Canadian theatre. I know that the work of her mature years would have been as noteworthy, and a futher addition to Canadian drama.

Pamela Hawthorn
Vancouver, B.C.
August, 1987

JENNIE'S STORY

Jennie's Story was first produced by the New Play Centre at the Canadian Theatre Today Conference in Saskatoon, Saskatchewan, and at the Waterfront Theatre in Vancouver, B.C., in October, 1981, with the following cast:

JENNIE McGrane	*Sherry Bie*
HARRY McGrane	*Pierre Tetrault*
FATHER Edward Fabrizeau	*David Ferry*
EDNA Delevault	*Lillian Carlson*
MOLLY Dorval	*Laura Bruneau*

Directed by Jace van der Veen.
Stage Managed by Paddy McEntee.

Jennie's Story was subsequently produced by the CentreStage Company at the St. Lawrence Centre in Toronto, in April, 1983, with the following cast:

JENNIE McGrane	*Nora McLellan*
HARRY McGrane	*Michael Hogan*
FATHER Edward Fabrizeau	*William Mockridge*
EDNA Delevault	*Clare Coulter*
MOLLY Dorval	*Denise Naples*

Directed by Bill Glassco.
Designed by Sue Le Page.
Stage Managed by Catherine Russell.

The Characters

JENNIE McGrane *about 21 or 22*
HARRY McGrane *about 35 to 39*
FATHER Edward Fabrizeau *about 35 to 39*
EDNA Delevault *Jennie's mother, about 48*
MOLLY Dorval *age 15*

The Setting

The McGrane farm, in the house. There is a kitchen, a porch, an upstairs bedroom. There is a door to the porch, and one to the pantry. A hallway leads to the upstairs and the front room.

The Time

1938-39.

Author's Notes

For the legal background for this play, see "The Sexual Sterilization Act" (Alberta, 1928), especially Section 5, which concerns "multiplication of the evil by the transmission of the disability to progeny." In 1937, just before the time of the play, an amendment was passed, making it possible to sterilize a person without his or her consent, provided consent was given by the appropriate relative or, if the appropriate relative did not exist or was not resident in Alberta, by the Minister of Health. This law was repealed in 1971.

A similar law existed in British Columbia from 1928 to 1973. Also, sterilization is apparently still being performed in the United Kingdom on the "socially unfit" (see The Observer, *April 5, 1981, page 6, "The Victims of Britain's Secret Sterilizations").*

See also the 1972 white paper on "Protection of Life," working paper 24, chairman Francis C. Muldoon.

The author of the poetry used in the play is Gerard Manley Hopkins.

In Act One, Scene Four, the characters use a "waxing brick." This is a brick wrapped in flannel, used as a buffer.

The "Indian rings" referred to in the play are found in southern Alberta, and also in Saskatchewan, along the river, on buttes. As Harry says in the play, they are often found one day's canoe trip apart. Archaeologists guess the age of the circles to be perhaps 100,000 years, and, because of the placement of larger boulders, that they were used as an almanac of some kind.

Act One, Scene One

*We first see the bedroom. JENNIE is
lighting a kerosene lamp. She stretches like
a cat. She gets out of bed unhurriedly,
putting on HARRY's slippers. Then she
puts on HARRY's kimono, which is much
too large for her. Her hair hangs loose about
her head. It is fiery, almost red, and curly;
tendrils escape like halo flashes. Although
her hair spreads about her face like a halo,
there is nothing of the madonna in
JENNIE—everything she does is sensuous.
She is a woman at one with her body. Now
she smells the kimono, the smell of
HARRY. She straightens the bed covers,
spreading and then folding back the quilt,
ready for HARRY in case he should come
back to bed. Now she takes the kerosene
lamp and comes down into the hall and then
into the kitchen. At the entrance to the
kitchen she looks at the electric switch, and
then up to the bulb hanging from the middle
of the ceiling. Emboldened, mischievous,
she almost switches it on, then, scared, does
not. She puts the kerosene lamp on the
table, goes to the first of the two doors,
opens it, and looks out toward the
bunkhouse. Now she comes back to the
range and moves the kettle to the hot part of
the top. The range dominates the kitchen.
It is big and black and shiny with stove
blacking. It is always on. In general, the*

kitchen has a sense of sparse, spare, house-proud prosperity. There is a sink with a pump attached—very advanced for this time. There are electric wires running up and down the walls—hence the electric light. There is a wooden table, scrubbed bone-white. There is a big leather armchair, placed so HARRY can look out the door. A book rack is beside it, with a very few old leather books. The door has two doors—in winter there is a storm door and in summer there is a screen door. JENNIE lays a starched embroidered table cloth on the table. Now she goes to the pantry and brings back a tray of teacups, saucers, plates, etc.—the best china. She starts to go back to the pantry for the pie but then stops. Billy White has just died.

JENNIE   Domine Jesu Christem Rex gloriae, libera anima omnium fidelium defunctorum de paenis inferni and from the deep pit. Deliver him from the lion's mouth, that Hell may not swallow him up and may he not fall into darkness, but may the holy standard-bearer, Michael, lead him into the holy light. ...poor old Billy.

Now JENNIE goes into the pantry to get the pie, heavy cream, sugar, etc., all quite casually, in spite of the prayer she has just said for the dead. As she comes back, she thinks of Billy's old dog.

Poor Tuffy, poor old thing.

Offstage, two men are heard coming up to the porch—HARRY McGrane and FATHER Edward Fabrizeau. The FATHER is in a navy blue heavy wool overcoat, black suit, and a collar. He wears slip-on rubbers over oxford shoes. HARRY is wearing jeans,

> *plaid shirt, a windbreaker, a farmer's cap, and*
> *wellington rubbers, which he carefully wipes*
> *on a boot scraper outside the door. As*
> *HARRY comes in he takes off the*
> *wellingtons and stands them on a piece of*
> *paper. The FATHER, however, goes to the*
> *table and sits. HARRY peels off his*
> *windbreaker. The FATHER stays hot and*
> *sweaty in his overcoat.*

HARRY (*over the above*) Didn't I say she'd be ready?
(*laughs*) Didn't I say she'd know? Jennie always
knows. She's like an old pagan lady, my Jennie.
I bet she knew before Tuffy did, didn't you,
Jennie?

> *JENNIE is getting the tea ready. No sense*
> *of urgency. For instance, she warms the*
> *teapot against her own body, liking the feel*
> *of the heat, before she empties the pot and*
> *puts tea leaves in. Now she gets a bucket*
> *from the cupboard under the sink, pours*
> *some lye in, gets a rag from under the sink.*

Oh oh, here she comes in her lye'n'water, goingta
wipe up your footprints, Father. Shoulda warned
you, take off your rubbers you enter Jennie's
kingdom.

> *JENNIE wipes up the wet marks from the*
> *FATHER's rubbers.*

JENNIE (*pleased*) Oh Harry.

HARRY No, she knew before Tuffy did even. Like a cat.
Cats know first, Father. Then dogs. I said to the
Father, here, you watch now, Jennie'll have
something on the table for us, soon's we come
in, didn't I, Father?

FATHER   What's that smell?

HARRY   That's Jennie an' her damn lye water, always cleaning. I bet I've got the cleanest outhouse the whole parish.

FATHER   It must burn the hands.

JENNIE   (*wrings out the cloth, puts bucket back under sink, hangs cloth up*) Would you like some pie then?

FATHER   Like a hospital. It smells like a hospital in here.

HARRY   (*sits down at his place at the table*) Pie'd go good. Don't sit there in your coat, Father, you'll get all hot and sweaty and catch your death your way home.

         HARRY *gets up again, helps the* FATHER *out of his coat, and hangs it on back of the third chair. He blows out expansively as he sits down—a long hard night over at last.* JENNIE *starts to cut the pie, then pours milk into the* FATHER's *cup.*

FATHER   I don't take milk any more.

JENNIE   Oh, sorry. You allus took milk in first before.

FATHER   I don't now.

JENNIE   (*picks up teacup*) Well, I kin throw it out.

HARRY   I'll take it, Jen, not to waste it.

JENNIE   No, I'll throw it out. You got your own cup.

         JENNIE *takes the* FATHER's *cup to the sink, pours it out, rinses it in water, dries it*

    on a tea towel, comes back, pours tea into
    it. Then, she pours milk in HARRY's *cup,*
    then tea. Everything is done with a
    slowness and a sureness—HARRY *enjoys*
    watching her. The FATHER *watches her*
    with frustration and exasperation.

HARRY   Won't hafta wait anyways.

JENNIE   No, that's right. Won't have to wait. (*serves*
    HARRY *a piece of pie*)

HARRY   That's one good thing, Father. Won't hafta wait
    if the Chinook holds. 'd never feel right going in
    fer Communion knowin' ol' Billy's out back in
    the woodshed waitin' for the thaw. (*laughs*)

    FATHER *looks down and cannot speak.*

    Aw come on, Father. Old Billy was ready to go.

JENNIE   (*hovering at the pie plate, ready to serve*
    FATHER *a slice*) He was 86, Father.

HARRY   'n' if he wasn't ready, he shoulda bin! (*laughs,*
    starts to eat his pie)

JENNIE   (*indicating big stoneware jug with a wooden*
    spoon standing up in it) There's heavy cream.

HARRY   Heavy cream'd go nice, heavy cream'd go good.

    JENNIE *ladles the cream onto* HARRY's
    pie. He indicates more. They laugh at each
    other for their gluttony. JENNIE *and*
    HARRY *never overtly touch in this scene,*
    but, in their laughter, we know how alive
    each is to the other.

FATHER   Why was he so afraid to die? He'd done nothin',
    nothin'!

HARRY	(*eating*) Maybe that's why. I mean, look at it this way, Father, imagine goin' an' nothin' on yer conscience. (*laughs*)
	FATHER *looks away.*
	I mean, what'd there be to talk about! Father, a man without sin ain't human. Isn't that right?
JENNIE	He wasn't scared this afternoon. I played Hearts with him all afternoon.
HARRY	Eat some pie, Father. Sit down with us, Jen, go on.
JENNIE	No, my mother never sat down with her men, and I'll not start. I'll see to my dough.
	JENNIE *goes to the warming oven, takes out a bowl of dough, takes it to the kneading table, sprinkles flour, kneads and pokes dough, etc. When she is through, she covers it with a clean tea cloth and puts it back in the warming oven. Conversation continues through the above actions.*
HARRY	'n' they say Black Irish is bad. In my house, Jennie, you can sit with the men! God, these Frenchies! I will speak with your mother, Jennie.
JENNIE	She never sat down with her men.
HARRY	Have some pie. Father, you got a long drive back. (*pause*) I'll clean him up for you first. (*to* JENNIE) You got boiler water hot?
JENNIE	Yes.
HARRY	(*helps* FATHER *to a slice of pie*) Eat up, Father.

Drink your tea. (*pause*) Come to think on it, old Billy had lots on his conscience.

FATHER   Nothin' venial. Nothin' mortal.

HARRY   You call his singing in choir nothin' venial, Father? I call old Billy's voice in choir venial, Father, venial at the least.

         JENNIE *chuckles.*

(*an edge of steel in his voice*) Drink up your tea, Father, while it's still hot.

FATHER   You find everythin' amusin', Harry.

HARRY   And you take things too serious, Eddie Fabrizeau, and allus did. (*pause*) Sorry. I mean, *Father.* Father, old Billy was old and he was tired and he was bored. It was time.

FATHER   He died afraid on me!

HARRY   (*pause*) You had to give him his last rites. That's your job. When a man hears the last rites, he's bound to get scared. For a bit. It's nothin' you can help.

FATHER   But just before, he was jokin' with you, laughin' with you.

HARRY   Hell, Father, I'm Irish. Here, Jennie, why'n't you turn on the light. (*gets up, goes to switch beside door to hallway, turns on electric light bulb*) Here, Father, look at this. (*turns it off, turns it on again*) Jennie won't touch it. Scared to get a shock.

FATHER   Electricity? You got electricity in, Harry?

HARRY   Damn right. And it's indoor plumbing next. I got it in upstairs too, in our bedroom, and the small room. For when it's needed.

                         HARRY *looks at* JENNIE. *She smiles, looks down.*

               I meant to string it out to the bunkhouse, fer old Billy. But he come in yesterday. I carried him in. He saw it.

JENNIE   Oh, he got such a kick, Father. He lay there like a big baby in Harry's arms. And he did it hisself, he turned it on, he turned it off. He was *laughin'*! Fit to beat the band.

HARRY   He never let up about it all night neither. He kept sayin', "Where's the light, Harry?" 'cause see (*to* FATHER) I'd promised him electricity out to the bunkhouse and, jeez, he never forgot nothin', old Billy. "Where's the light, Harry?" (*laughs*)

FATHER   "Where's the light." Yes. I heard him. I thought he meant somethin' else.

HARRY   No! He was holdin' me to my word, see. 'cause I said I'd string out a wire ta the bunkhouse. "Where's the light, Harry?" (*laughs*) Hell, I'll hafta put a light bulb in the coffin, just for him, he'll curse me from the grave else. (*comes back to the table*)

                         JENNIE *pours more tea.*

               (*turns the kerosene lamp down, then blows it out*) Don't need no kerosene no more, Jen. (*pause*) Here, give us some more a that pic. Nothin' like a dyin' to give a man an appetite!

FATHER *puts his face in his hands.*

(*embarrassment, tinged with disgust*) Git the
man a handkerchief, Jen.

> JENNIE *goes into the pantry where the
> laundry basket is kept, comes back with
> unironed handkerchief and gives it to the
> FATHER.*

JENNIE It's not ironed. I'm sorry.

> FATHER *puts handkerchief to his face, tries
> to control himself.*

HARRY We kin bury him Wednesday.

JENNIE Yes, and if the Chinook holds, we can get in too,
this time. I got a new hat.

FATHER (*viciously*) You got a new hat!

HARRY Here, Father.

FATHER And you got electricity. And indoor plumbing
next. You've done well for yourself, Jennie
Delevault.

HARRY Yes, we've done good, Father, ever since you
married us. Jennie McGrane and me.

FATHER Billy White just died in your bunkhouse. I
should think you'd have a prayer to say for his
soul.

JENNIE Oh I did it already.

FATHER (*pause*) What?

JENNIE I said it already, before I got the pie out.

FATHER   But you didn't know then.

HARRY   Jennie knew. (*reminding her*) I'll have some
                more a that pie, Jen.

                        JENNIE *cuts more pie, ladles cream, but she
                        is rattled.*

FATHER   How could she know?

JENNIE   Old Billy, he liked the electric light. He said it
                was warm. He said he could feel it warming his
                bones. He hated the cold. He was allus so cold,
                this last winter. I don't like to think of him in
                the ground. Will you really, Harry?

HARRY   Yes.

JENNIE   I mean promise not teasin'.

HARRY   I will put a light bulb in Billy's coffin.
                (*sideways grin at the* FATHER) When no one's
                lookin'.

FATHER   (*pause*) The whole district hailed out last summer
                except for you. The whole country in a black
                depression and you get a new truck and electricity
                and *you* (*to* JENNIE) get a new hat. (*suddenly
                laughs*)

HARRY   That's right, ever since you married us, Jennie's
                brought me nothin' but luck.

FATHER   The ony luck is the Devil's luck! The grace a
                God is not luck, Harry.

HARRY   Well, you know, Father, it is a funny thing all
                right. We're ony farm you didn't bless crop on,
                and we're ony farm doesn't get hailed out. Maybe
                you're a hoodoo.

FATHER   What?

JENNIE   He's ony teasin', Father. Harry teases somethin' awful.

HARRY   (*eating his pie*) No, but it's true all the same. Give us another dollop that heavy cream, Jen. There you tuk off, up to that retreat you went to, soon's you married me and Jennie, and you never gave my crop the blessing. Give ever'body's else the blessing but not mine. And here I stand, hailstorm all around me, grace a God shinin' down, right along the concession line. I mean, true to God, Father, you never saw nothin' like. Old Bailey's farm? Right acrost barbed wire? Big dark purple clouds. Hailstones big as baseballs, whole wheatfield bent flat. I could see it, but my section, sun shinin' away, grasshoppers hoppin', birds singin', like a door in the sky opened up and God said, "save the McGrane place," and all else damn them to Hell. Good thing I'm not an ignorant Black Irish Catholic, Father, or I'd think you're a hoodoo.

FATHER   That's blasphemy, Harry McGrane, you'll confess to blasphemy Friday night. For Easter.

HARRY   That's teasin', Eddie Fabrizeau, that's teasin' get you outa bad mood. (*pause*) Look, sorry. Father. I *mean* to say Father. Billy White just died. It's true he died hard. Sometimes men die hard. But now, look at it this way, old Billy's gone to heaven, a good man and a good Catholic, but a bad bass, never sang a clear note in church, but bound for the heavenly choir, good pitch and true voice at last!

JENNIE   And now poor Tuffy'll die too.

FATHER   What?

HARRY His dog. Billy's dog.

JENNIE Now he'll die. He'll mourn and he'll die.

HARRY (*getting up*) Well, I guess it's time. You get the washbasin, girl.

> JENNIE *goes and gets a big washbasin and ladles out the hot water from the boiler in the range. She gets soap and a towel.*

Don't give me nothin' good, you want to use later, Billy wouldn't mind.

JENNIE Harry! I'd never.

> HARRY *puts on his windbreaker and boots as* JENNIE *hands him the basin.*

HARRY You di'n't put none a yer lye in this, did ya?

JENNIE (*laughs*) Oh, *Harry.*

HARRY Wouldn't want old Bill's skin burnt off *afore* he gets to the Judgement Seat. I mean, might prejudice the case, might predetermine the jury.

JENNIE Oh, you're awful.

HARRY "Here, Billy," says God, "what'd ya do, take a detour on yer way up? Devil singe yer butt?"

> JENNIE *and* HARRY *laugh together, a gentle, sad laugh.*

FATHER I'll help you. (*does not move from his chair*)

HARRY No...you anointed him. Now I'll wash him. You stay and eat yer pie. Jennie makes a good pie. You eat up, Father.

HARRY *turns and goes out. He stands for a*
moment on the porch, not looking back.
Now we see how tired he is and how aware
of the two people he has left alone in the
room behind him. Now he leaves for the
bunkhouse. JENNIE *and the* FATHER *are*
quiet.

JENNIE   It's the thought a the grave, I think. So dark and
lonesome. And cold. Why he was scared.
Sometimes even animals get scared at the end,
Father.

FATHER   We are not animals.

JENNIE   (*pause*) Harry says the best a us got some animal
in us somewheres. I'd be scared too. I mean, it's
a dark 'n' empty hole, i'n't it? I wouldn't like it
neither, not without Harry.

FATHER   You said a prayer before you *knew*? (*pause*)
What prayer?

JENNIE   Oh Father, I'll get it all wrong, front of you.

FATHER   *What prayer!*

JENNIE   Domine Jesu Christe, Rex gloriacm Libera
animas omnium fidelium defunctorum...

JENNIE *continues the speech, until the*
FATHER *cuts her off.*

FATHER   Close yer robe, woman! (*pause*) That lye is
ruinin' yer hands. They're all red 'n' cracked.

JENNIE   I use vaseline.

FATHER   They all die afraid on me. And nobody wants me
to do the blessing. I never blessed Harry's crop

an' Harry's ony one doesn't get hailed out. It's a
blasphemy. A priest can't be a hoodoo.

JENNIE Harry's only teasin', Father. Harry's against
superstition.

FATHER Harry's Black Irish, all Black Irish are
superstitious. It's Harry's been spreadin' I'm a
hoodoo.

JENNIE No. No, truly, Father. No...Harry ony says yer
a scourge.

FATHER What?

JENNIE It's a good word, i'n't it? Harry knows lots of
good words. (*tastes the word*) A *scourge*. A
scourge. It's what I say now, I go to clean the
outhouse. "I'll scourge *you*," I say. (*chuckles;
pause*) See, old Billy didn't want you, it's true.
But Harry stuck up for you, he says, "No, Billy,
we need the priest for dyin' and bornin' and
marryin' even if he's a scourge." So you see?
Harry sticks up for you. Please eat somethin',
Father, you look so peaked.

FATHER You poor simple woman.

JENNIE Please, Father, I worry for you, you look so
kinda shadowy now. I worry for you without me
to do for you.

FATHER Mrs. Day does perfectly well for me.

JENNIE Mrs. Day! Mrs. Day's past her prime, Mrs. Day
can't *see* dirt in *front* of her, everybody knows
Mrs. Day's not clean.

FATHER Clean? You dare to talk to me about *clean*?
Close your robe! (*pause*) Mrs. Day does me

fine. She's a good woman.

JENNIE   Well, her pastry's never nothin' like mine. Go
            on, eat up. I worry for you.

FATHER   Your hair's down.

JENNIE   (*starts to braid her hair in one long braid*) Well, I
            allus took it out at night, Father. 'n' I allus
            braids it up hard 'n' tight in the mornin', ony, it
            gets out, it escapes me, n' matter what I do.
            Harry says it's just my nature, my hair leaps out
            like shining. (*small laugh*) There. It's back
            proper now.

FATHER   I'm a bad priest an' all for your sake.

JENNIE   But that's all over now, Father. (*pause*) You said
            that was all over. I confessed and did my
            penance, so that's all over. Harry says you got to
            trust to God's infinite mercy.

FATHER   Yes. (*pause*) You swore you'd never tell. You
            swore.

JENNIE   'n' I never! Ony, at first, you see, I was ascared a
            bit. I mean, when it was Harry an' me, it seemed
            to come over me again, all what'd happened, so I
            cried some at first, and that's not in my nature,
            Father. Cryin' is not in my nature, as you well
            know.

FATHER   You was allus singin'.

JENNIE   Well, I never knew then, did I?

FATHER   That terrible winter. I had to make a tunnel to
            the church. Like an underground cave. I'd go
            into the church and lie on the cold stone, my
            arms stretched out like my Blessed Lord on the

cross, and through the cave of snow to the
rectory, I would hear you. Singin'.

JENNIE So one day, Harry takes me on his knee and he
says, "What's this then, Jen?" an' I never said
nothin', only what I *did* say was, I wished I was
dead. So Harry hit me.

FATHER Hit you?

JENNIE Harry says that was the worst thing a person
could ever say and I was never to say it again, it
was despair, and that's the worst sin of all of
them. And then (*smiles*) he said some poem
about cows. Just to make me laugh.

FATHER God forgive you.

JENNIE Oh he has, Father, and God has too. Well,
anyways, what he did was, see, he picked me up
and he carried me right out there to the porch.
(*crosses to the door, looks out toward bunkhouse*)
An' he says this poem about *cows*. (*laughs*) I
kin say part a it, too. See, he picks me up in his
arms—good thing Harry's a big strong man!
—an' he takes me to the door and he kicks open
the door—it was spring then, seeding time, so we
ony had screen door on—and he says, "Glory be
to God for dappled things." (*laughs*) Fer skies as
cupple coloured as a brinded cow. That's a Jersey,
I think, Father. A brinded cow's like a Jersey, the
kind they got over to Dora's Bob's place. So
anyways, *I* can't help laughin' an' I says, "What
kind a poem is that anyways, Harry McGrane, a
poem about cows?!" An' Harry says, "It's the
best kind a poem and I was not ever again to
worry no more about sin because what we did
together wasn't no sin and God had blessed our
bodies and we was goingta make skies as cupple
coloured as a brinded cow together, an' if he ever

heard me measlin' on again, he'd give me
another'd send me to Lumbreck and right over the
Crow's Nest. 'n' he meant it too. (*pause*) So,
anyways, I gave it up. I mean, I gave up
measlin', and took back my own nature.

FATHER   It's a poem by a priest.

JENNIE   Is it? I never knew that. I never knew a priest
knew nothin' about cows.

FATHER   My father had range cattle. I was born a farm
boy. I'd've had my dad's place by now, up to the
Porcupines.

> JENNIE *clears away the* FATHER's
> *untouched pie and other things. She goes to*
> *the pantry, and comes back.*

JENNIE   (*nervously*) Father? The thing is, I done my
penance, and I do trust to God's infinite mercy,
ony nothin's still happening. So, now I got you
here, could I ask, Father, if you wouldn't mind, I
beg your pardon, but see, Father, it's been a
whole year we're married, Harry 'n' me, and
nothin' happenin' still, and see, I understood, like,
when I was doin' fer you at the rectory, but now
it's Harry, see, and Harry's my husband. And so,
Father, what I got to know is, have you
confessed?

FATHER   What do you mean, you "understand" how it was
at the rectory?

JENNIE   Well, how nothin' ever happened. I mean, that
was God's mercy wa'n't it?

FATHER   (*bitter laugh*) You don't realize what you've done
to me, you poor stupid woman. (*pause*) When I
was a boy the priest who came to the Porcupines

was like a prince. He came only twice a year. He was like a prince of the Church, like a king. My mother cried when I went away to the seminary. I said, "Don't cry, Ma, I'll crown your head with glory." But Harry's right. I'm just an old plowhorse, takin' them down inta death or up inta life, or to the marriage bed. A gelding. My people despise me.

JENNIE   But Father, Harry 'n' me—

FATHER   Harry and you, Harry and you!

JENNIE   (*stubbornly*) 'n' nothin' happenin' yet!

FATHER   (*furious*) Even our Lord lost his temper once! Even Jesus blasted the fig tree!

JENNIE   Father?

FATHER   Harry *knows*! Harry knows and he's destroyed me with my own people.

JENNIE   But I never told him Father, never.

FATHER   Ahhhh. You told him, Jennie.

JENNIE   No, I never! I never! 'n' I kin prove it too!

FATHER   It's quite clear Harry knows.

JENNIE   No. Because if Harry knew—

FATHER   He knows, whatever you swear, and the oath of an imbecile is worth nothin'. I knew that, God help me, I knew that.

JENNIE   (*simply*) I kin prove Harry don't know, Father. Because if Harry did know, he'd kill you.

> HARRY *comes back to the porch. He puts the basin, soap, and dirty towelling down. He looks to the east, stretches, and yawns. Now he scrapes off his wellingtons, and comes in. He takes off his boots, wind-breaker, etc., and hangs his windbreaker and cap on a wooden peg behind the door. He walks over to his place by the table. JENNIE makes a gesture with the teapot as if to ask, "More tea?", but he shakes his head. A small, awkward silence.*

HARRY   Well, Billy White's in back a yer Dodge, Father. Took me longer'n I thought. He'd leaked a bit.

> HARRY *looks from* JENNIE*'s suffused face to the* FATHER*'s apoplectic one. He is sizing up what must have been going on.*

Well, he's clean as a baby now. Should be okay 'til ya get him back in the woodshed. Got quite a smile on his face now, if you want to take a look. 'course that's the stiffenin'. (*pause*) Still, we kin allus pretend, can't we?

> *The* FATHER *pushes back his chair, gets up, and starts for the door. He turns back, gets his coat from the other chair, and struggles into it.* HARRY *does not help him.*

JENNIE   (*finally*) Let me help you, Father—

FATHER   No!

HARRY   Anyways, Father, do me a favour. Don't fergit ta close old Bailey's gate top a the pasture. You forgot ta close the cattle gate th'other day, his cows was all down my side there, old Bailey was madder'n hell.

FATHER   I did not forget to close Joe Bailey's gate. I'm a farmer's son. I never forget to close a cattle gate.

HARRY   Whatever you say, Father, ony you was last out, and the cows got out, all down my side, and ol' Bailey, he was fit to be tied.

FATHER   I'll set the funeral for Wednesday.

HARRY   We'll be there. If the weather holds.

FATHER   (*turns from the door*) I will bless this house.

> JENNIE *and* HARRY *suddenly become still.*

I will bless this house, or are you an ignorant Black Irish Catholic, Harry McGrane, believing in hoodoos?

HARRY   (*pause*) Right, Father, right. You bless our house. Put yer back inta her.

> HARRY *and* JENNIE *kneel. The* FATHER *places a hand on each head.*

FATHER   Denedicat vos omnipotens, Deus, Pater et Filius et Spiritus Sanctus. Amen. (*makes the sign of the cross*)

JENNIE   (*frightened*) Amen.

HARRY   Amen.

FATHER   And I'll see you both for Easter Confession. Friday.

HARRY   If the weather still holds.

> HARRY *holds the door open for the* FATHER. *The* FATHER *goes out, crosses*

the porch, and exits.

(*calling after him*) Listen! If old Billy sits up
back a the seat while you're drivin' him home,
don't worry! It's ony nature! (*laughs; steps out
onto the porch, breathing in the soft morning air*)
"...the Holy Ghost over the bent
World broods with warm breast and with ah!
bright wings." (*pause*) There, that should take
the curse off. There's nothin' like a good
Chinook. Whole world smells good. (*pause*)
We got us a whole half hour to kill.

JENNIE *laughs.*

(*coming back in and shutting the door*) Well,
there it is, Jen, here we got us a whole half hour
ta do with and nothin' ta do with ourselves.
God's given us a whole half hour holiday between
work and sunup.

JENNIE

(*mock innocent*) I could get my bread in.

HARRY *chases her.* JENNIE *pretends to
run away. Finally he pulls her up and
around his body and carries her into the
hallway and up into the bedroom.*

Act One, Scene Two

*Harvest time. Now there is a screen door on
the kitchen doorway leading to the porch. It
is about nine o'clock in the morning.
EDNA Delevault is scouring pots and pans
at the sink, although they do not need
scouring. She is a brisk, round woman.
She wears a starched house dress that
crackles and snaps, and, on top of this, a*

> *brightly patterned, highly starched bib apron
> that ties at the back. Her braided hair is in a
> net. She wears lisle stockings and proper
> black lace-up shoes. Superficially EDNA is
> frustrated as she bangs the pots about, but
> underneath she is afraid. It is threshing
> time, and the kitchen should have the
> appearance of lavish preparation of food:
> pies, muffins, vegetables, roasting pans.
> The range is red hot. JENNIE comes in
> from the hallway, dressed to go to town.
> Her hair is braided in two braids and is coiled
> at the back of her head, but those tendrils
> escape and frame her face. She too is
> wearing highly polished oxford lace-ups, but
> also silk stockings and a two-piece suit, very
> neat, but somehow sensual as well. She
> carries a hat box, a pair of gloves, and a
> black patent leather purse. She is wearing
> pearls. She sets the box down and puts on
> some clip-on pearl earrings.*

EDNA   You're ready then.

JENNIE   Almost.

EDNA   Takin' time from Harry's work.

JENNIE   It ony takes Harry 'n hour to drive me to the
              train. With the new truck.

EDNA   Threshing time. (*banging away at the pots, pans
              and muffin tins*)

JENNIE   There's never a *good* time, Ma. 'n' this way I
              won't get snowed in. Best time to go *is* winter
              but the train could get snowed in and I'd be away
              for weeks, months, like it happened that year.

EDNA   (*stops her pot-banging; grumpily*) How long
              it'll take then.

JENNIE   Well, I figure ony two days. Then I'll be back.

                EDNA *comes over, starts to fix* JENNIE'*s
                hair, to push back the fly-away strands.*

                Day to go, day to see the doctor, day to visit with
                Mrs. Finlay, and do a bit of shopping—Harry's
                got me a list—and a day to come back.

EDNA   That's four days. I make that four days.

JENNIE   Well, I meant ony two days *there*, Ma.

EDNA   Puttin' Mrs. Finlay out.

JENNIE   Mrs. Finlay don't mind.

EDNA   How you had the gall, write to Mrs. Finlay and
                her United Church.

JENNIE   I did fer her first, Ma, and you was pleased
                enough about it at the time, United 'r not.

EDNA   (*slightly mollified*) I trained you right, it's true.
                Mrs. Finlay said she never had a cleaner girl do
                for her. (*pause*) It's not in yer nature to do this,
                Jennie. Not in yer nature. In threshin' time.
                You was always so...biddable. But now you get
                this bit in yer teeth and it's all self self self. I
                don't know you anymore.

JENNIE   The doctor said, "Come now," so I'm comin'
                now.

EDNA   Don't think I'm touchin' that electricity. Never
                mind, maybe you got some sort a shock, that's
                what I think, playin' with nature like that. Yes,
                that's what I think, you got some sorta shock
                from all the electricity Harry's puttin' in.
                Machines ta milk cows, what next, they'll all go

up in smoke, you'll see. (*begins to scour another pot*)

JENNIE   (*mildly*) You needn't do that, Ma. Harry's bringin' the Dorval girl.

EDNA   Never mind about no Dorval girl. The Dorvals were never clean.

JENNIE   Oh Ma! (*laughs*) Lucy Dorval, she come to the rectory once, run her finger on plate ledge to see if I'd dusted. Wearing white gloves, mind. It's her girl Harry's bringin'.

EDNA   (*pause*) I hope you'd dusted it.

JENNIE   Ony 15, but a willin' worker, Harry says. Oh yeah, it was clean. White gloves. Was *she* disappointed. (*laughs*)

EDNA   Well, *I* never asked for no Dorval girl. I cooked for threshers before.

JENNIE   Unh uh, now Ma, you went on enough about it when I asked you in the first place. So Harry says, we'll get in the Dorval girl, so that's an end to that.

EDNA   (*suddenly putting her face in her apron and almost beginning to cry*) Oh Jennie.

JENNIE   (*frightened*) Ma? Ma, what is it? (*does not move toward* EDNA) I got to go, Ma, don't make me cry, Ma. The doctor's goingta fix ever'thin'.

EDNA   (*controls herself, blows her nose*) I don't hold with no doctors pokin'.

JENNIE   He saved my life that time.

EDNA   You never had no appendix.

JENNIE   Oh Ma!…ever'body's got appendix.

EDNA   Not you. I never held with that. Tearin' off to
            that place, tearin' off for *appendix.*

            > JENNIE *takes her hat out of the hat box. It*
            > *is a straw with a ribbon, very chic for the*
            > *time. She puts it on, with a hat pin, and*
            > *looks over* EDNA's *shoulder into the mirror*
            > *above the sink.*

JENNIE   The doctor's ony goingta *look*, Ma, and he's the
            same doctor was there then, is why I wrote to
            him first place.

EDNA   Well, do what you want. You will anyhow. But
            it's not like you, Jennie, that's all I will say. It's
            all self self self with you now.

JENNIE   Oh Ma. (*pauses, turning*) Well? What about the
            hat then?

EDNA   It's all right.

JENNIE   All right!!

EDNA   What did that set Harry back?

JENNIE   (*proud, knowing the shock this will cause*) Four
            dollars—

EDNA   Four…dollars…

JENNIE   —an' fifty cents! (*looks at herself again in the*
            mirror)

EDNA   You oughta be ashamed of yourself. Four dollars
            and…four dollars and fifty cents. It's ony a bit of

	straw and a bit of veil, I coulda made it for nothin'.
JENNIE	Harry says you pay for the style.
EDNA	Harry spoils you. He spoils you rotten. (*pause*) Four dollars and fifty cents. And payin' that Dorval girl what?
JENNIE	Dollar a day.
EDNA	Dollar a day *and* all found? Dollar a day and all *found*?! (*pause*) Did ya get it at Mademoiselle Rose's?
JENNIE	Ummmm Hmm.
EDNA	(*awed*) I never even bin in Mademoiselle Rose's.
JENNIE	'n' after harvest, Harry's takin' me back, get a new winter coat with a fox fur collar. And a muff!
EDNA	At Mademoiselle Rose's?
JENNIE	MMM mmm.
EDNA	I'd be scared to go inside Mademoiselle Rose's.
JENNIE	Harry says they don't care who comes in, they got money to pay. Come in in your apron.
EDNA	(*laughs*) It does look nice though, I have to admit it. (*pause*) Oh, Jennie, it's just, I lost five children before they was a year, and then my Ben. Now there's ony you.
JENNIE	(*moves to her, takes her hand*) The doctor's not goingta kill me, Ma. He's ony goingta look.
EDNA	It's God's will, Jennie.

JENNIE   (*becoming exasperated, pauses*) There's Harry at the bridge now.

EDNA   If she don't use lye with her scrub water, she's outa this place.

      JENNIE's gift for hearing things is so common, EDNA doesn't even bother to comment on the fact that the bridge is some distance away.

JENNIE   I got good soap, Ma. Lye's hard on the skin. It burns yer hands.

EDNA   I knew I couldn't find it. I looked ever'where!

JENNIE   I gave up lye in the spring.

EDNA   (*shocked*) You don't have lye in this place?

JENNIE   Not since the spring. I give it up. Makes place smell like hospital.

EDNA   Lye burns away the filth—Harry'll hafta go into Gifford's he's in town, I'll never feel safe else.

JENNIE   You won't find no dirt, Ma.

EDNA   I'll find it. (*pause*) Does she dry iron? I won't have a girl doesn't dry iron.

JENNIE   Ma, I don't dry iron no more. It's easier sprinkle.

EDNA   You don't get to glory on ease. A good housewife uses lye in her scrub water to burn away the filth.

JENNIE   Oh Ma.

EDNA   It's God's will, yer goin' against God's will!

JENNIE   (*finally blazes at her*) God's will? How can it be
                God's will I don't have a baby?

EDNA   Oh!

                > EDNA *is near tears.* JENNIE *has never*
                > *spoken to her like this before.*

JENNIE   Here's Harry now. I'm sorry, Ma, but you go *on*.

                > JENNIE *goes to the screen door and waves.*
                > *Then she goes out to the porch. She calls*
                > *back, softly.*

                And the Dorval girl, Ma. My, she's a pretty one.

HARRY   (*off*) We're here.

JENNIE   (*coming down to the front of the porch*) Hello,
                hello! Hello, Molly!

                > HARRY *and* MOLLY *come up on the*
                > *porch.* HARRY *carries* MOLLY's *cardboard*
                > *valise for her.*

HARRY   Here's Miss Molly Dorval come to save the
                homestead!

                > MOLLY *giggles.* HARRY *has been*
                > *making her laugh all the 10 miles from the*
                > *Dorval place. They come into the kitchen,*
                > JENNIE *following.*

EDNA   You use lye in yer scrub water?

                > MOLLY *bursts into laughter.*

HARRY   (*taking valise into hallway*) I said you'd say that,
                Mother, right off, first thing, di'n't I, Molly?

EDNA   Well, I don't hold with a lick 'n' a polish.

HARRY   (*coming back into the kitchen*) Give the girl a chance, Mother, she just got in.

EDNA   Do you dry iron?

MOLLY   (*holding herself in*) My mother makes me dry iron, Mrs. Delevault. (*a quick conspiratorial glance at* HARRY; *a smothered laugh*)

> JENNIE, *at the door, notes this, and is slightly disturbed.*

EDNA   (*not satisfied*) Does she. Good fer yer mother. What about lye in yer scrub water? Harry? You get me lye to Gifford's you take Jennie in, they'll be open still, you get me a big can a lye to Gifford's...

> JENNIE *casts her eyes heavenwards.*

...charge it to *my* bill.

MOLLY   My ma puts lye in the outhouse.

EDNA   We put it in scrub water.

MOLLY   I got soft skin, Mrs. Delevault, it blisters real easy.

> EDNA *and* MOLLY *give each other a look now.* MOLLY *is not going to be a meek slave.* EDNA *grudgingly likes her for it.*

JENNIE   (*blurts out*) Makes house smell like hospital!

> *An awkward silence, awkward for everyone.*

HARRY   I'll just get my good jacket then. (*goes out the door to the hallway*)

EDNA   I trained my Jennie to do for people and I never had no complaints. My Jennie, she did for the United Church even, Mrs. Finlay up to Lumbreck. Mrs. Finlay said she never had such a clean girl do for her. Here, you want to be useful, you can do these spuds.

        EDNA *hands* MOLLY *a basin, a bucket of potatoes, and a paring knife.* MOLLY *sits down at the table and starts in.* HARRY *comes back in his other, better, windbreaker, carrying* JENNIE's *two-piece leather luggage set.*

HARRY   Got you to work already, has she? Yer a slavedriver, Mother.

        MOLLY *giggles.*

But her bite's much worse'n her bark, so stay away from her teeth.

        MOLLY *laughs outright.*

JENNIE   We got to *go*, Harry.

EDNA   And them's new too.

HARRY   This'n's called "overnight" bag, and this here's fer cosmetics.

EDNA   Jennie don't need no "cosmetics."

HARRY   Mmm, it's on her list, it's on her list.

JENNIE   Harry.

MOLLY | That's a real nice hat, you get that in Lethbridge? Mr. McGrane says yer goingta Calgary. I never even bin to Lethbridge. I never bin farrer'n Lumbreck, 'n' Porcupine Hills. They don't count though.

EDNA | Yer not being paid for conversation, Miss. Mind how yer goin'—that slice was this thick.

JENNIE | Why don't it count, Porcupine Hills, why don't Porcupine Hills count, it's farrer'n Lethbridge?

MOLLY | Oh that's my uncle's place, Charlie Fabrizeau's? It don't count you go to yer relatives, does it? I mean, it's not romantic nor nothin', just goingta yer relatives.

EDNA | Romantic!

JENNIE | That's right. Yer cousins to the Fabrizeaus.

MOLLY | Yeah, we're all related on my ma's side, my ma's a Fabrizeau.

JENNIE | Yer cousin to our priest.

MOLLY | Second cousin, once removed. We used to be in his parish too, but my ma won't go to him now, she says she'll never go to Father Fabrizeau, because he's cursed. This okay? (*holds potato up to* EDNA *for inspection*)

JENNIE | Why is he cursed?

EDNA | We don't hold with gossip this house.

> MOLLY *senses she may have overstepped. She looks from* EDNA's *face to* JENNIE's, *then to* HARRY's. HARRY *has turned away from her, and stands stiffly at the door.*

MOLLY   I don't know.

JENNIE   No, yer ma says Father Fabrizeau is cursed, why
               is he cursed?

MOLLY   (*a bit frightened at* JENNIE's *intensity*) I really
               don't know, Miz McGrane.

HARRY   We got to go, make that train.

JENNIE   Then why does yer ma say that?

MOLLY   I don't really know, Miz McGrane, all I know
               is—

EDNA   You better go, you want to catch yer train.

JENNIE   Be quiet, Ma.

MOLLY   (*lays down paring knife*) I shouldn'ha been
               listenin'. I was supposed to be in bed, but you
               can hear through floor. (*pause*) Well. My ma
               says it's because he didn't go to confession one
               winter. It was one winter he was snowed in. But
               he heard confession and he gave the mass. An' he
               was in mortal sin. (*pause*) That's what she said,
               Miz McGrane. But my da says it's just spite...
               he never married *her*, my da says Father Fabrizeau
               was real nice lookin' when he was young, and he
               says it's just spite, he married the Church instead
               of *her*. (*starts to laugh, then stops*) He's a tease,
               my da. Like Mister McGrane.

EDNA   I'll finish up them spuds. You kin go out 'n' take
               in the wash.

                    MOLLY *gets up obediently.* EDNA *hands
                    her the wicker basket from the pantry.*

               Mind pegs go in peg bag.

> *The peg bag would be on the line outside.*
> MOLLY *goes out. She is on the porch for a*
> *brief moment as she looks about her at the*
> *neat clean prosperous farm, and is pleased to*
> *be here. She exits.*

(*pause*) I don't want you to go, Jennie. Five babies I had, and all dead in the first year. And then Ben in the mine. You're all I have left.

JENNIE   Ma, don't start again.

EDNA   Mrs. Bailey, they cut her open, and she died.

JENNIE   You keep talkin' cuttin'.

EDNA   Riddled right through!

JENNIE   Mrs. Bailey had cancer, Ma.

EDNA   Holy Mary, Mother of God, don't send my Jennie to no doctor.

HARRY   Mother, they're not going to cut—

JENNIE   She keeps talkin' cuttin', why does she keep talkin' cuttin'?

HARRY   Mother, would I let anybody hurt our Jen?

JENNIE   It's the same doctor saved my *life*! You signed the paper.

> EDNA *slaps* JENNIE*'s face.* JENNIE *is*
> *astounded.*

HARRY   Here now, you'll be spankin' my woman next. Way you two carry on, a person'd think *you* was Black Irish. Mother? (*goes up to* EDNA, *puts his arm around her*) Mother? Now, the doctor's

ony goingta look at Jennie, see why she don't
start up. Now, don't blush. Mother, a woman
with seven children and you kin still blush. I
swear, I think a woman gets a virgin every
mornin' a her life.

HARRY *has misread* EDNA.

EDNA   Oh Harry.

HARRY   Now, you want a nice baby to nag and scold and
bully, don't you? 'n' you know no doctor can do
anythin' without I sign a paper.

EDNA *blows her nose. She tries to pull
herself back into some reasonable world, a
world in which she never signed a paper.*

EDNA   It's a wonder ya don't try fixin' her up yerself,
Harry McGrane, you and yer electricity!

HARRY   (*laughs*) Mother Delevault! Ah, now that's
somethin' not even a Black Irish can fix! Soo
now, soo.

HARRY *is still holding* EDNA, *and she
allows herself to be comforted.*

Now, Mother, soo. Would I do something to
hurt our Jen?

EDNA *shakes her head against his chest.*

Then trust to God, Mother Delevault. And if you
can't trust to God, trust to *me*. (*laughs*)

EDNA   (*pushes* HARRY *away*) Well, go on then, but
don't expect me ta touch them lights. It's
kerosene fer me 'til the day you git back, Jennie.

HARRY   (*picks up* JENNIE's *luggage*) Mmmm...mmm...
                 you wait 'n' see what Jen has fer you she comes
                 home. I'll convert you ta electricity yet!

EDNA   What? What infernity're you plannin' now,
                 Harry?

HARRY   (*moves to porch*) ...you wait 'n' see.

EDNA   (*moves toward* JENNIE) Now don't you go
                 throwin' away Harry's money.

JENNIE   (*forgiving*) Oh Ma.

HARRY   Don't say nothin', Jen. Let her be surprised.
                 Give her somethin' to chew on 'stead a Molly
                 Dorval, poor girl. (*laughs*)

                         HARRY *and* JENNIE *move out onto the*
                         porch.

JENNIE   'bye, Ma. God bless.

EDNA   God bless, Jennie.

                         HARRY *and* JENNIE *exit.*

MOLLY   (*off*) 'bye, Miz McGrane, 'bye, Mister McGrane!
                 'bye!

                         EDNA *stands very still for a moment. She*
                         closes her eyes, and crosses herself.
                         MOLLY *comes onto the porch with neatly*
                         folded laundry in the wicker basket. She
                         comes into the kitchen, sets the basket
                         down, and goes to the pantry door.

                 Iron in here?

EDNA   Yes. In pantry. Where else should it be?

> MOLLY *starts to go into the pantry.*

> No. Wait. No, it's on back a stove. I put it there myself. I'll lose my head next. It's ready, back a stove, hot. Ironin' *board's* in pantry.

> MOLLY *goes into the pantry, comes out with the ironing board, sees the light bulb, and then the switch.*

MOLLY   Gee! Mister McGrane's got electricity! Gee. (*goes to light switch*)

EDNA   Here, you leave that be.

MOLLY   (*switches lights on, off, on, off*) Gee! Look at that!

EDNA   (*without asperity*) That's enough a that, you want to wear it out? (*eyes MOLLY closely*) You call that folded? I don't call them sheets folded.

> EDNA *rips out a sheet and* MOLLY *gets on the other end, and they perform the age-old ballet of women folding sheets.* MOLLY *is expected to dry iron the sheets once they are folded properly. Over the next they work through sheets, table cloths.* EDNA *refolds tea towels, pillow cases, napkins.*

MOLLY   Mmm. I love the smell a fresh sheets. Like sunshine. Gee, this is a nice kitchen. Someday I'm goingta have a kitchen just like this. (*pause*) Now they got electric irons even. You just plug them in. Well, anyways, it won't be hard to dry iron these sheets.

> MOLLY *sets up one sheet on the ironing board, and goes to get the iron from the back*

> *of the stove. There should be two irons on the stove, one to use when the first gets cold.*

EDNA   And tea towels.

MOLLY   You dry iron tea towels too?

EDNA   This house, we do.

MOLLY   (*impressed*) Gee, even my ma don't dry iron tea towels.

EDNA   We don't hold with sprinkle.

MOLLY   No more does Ma.

EDNA   If you dry iron right off, fresh from the line, it's not so bad.

MOLLY   No.

EDNA   It's lazy housewives hafta sprinkle, 'cause they let ironing pile up. Do a job right away, you don't hafta sprinkle.

> MOLLY *tests the iron with spit, then irons the first sheet.*

Do your work as it comes up, you won't go wrong.

> MOLLY *continues ironing.* EDNA *folds one last tea towel.*

How far gone're ya?

MOLLY   (*startled, and then, in a moment, knows it's true*) Oh.

EDNA   Careful. You'll burn that sheet. (*takes the iron
                  from* MOLLY, *puts it back on iron rack on
                  stove*) Better sit down.

                      MOLLY *goes to the table, pulls out a chair,
                      and sits down.*

                  Didn't ya know?

                      MOLLY *shakes her head no.*

                  I'll make us a nice hot cup of tea. (*puts kettle
                  over the hot part of the range, waits for it to boil*)
                  You never knew then.

MOLLY   No. Not 'til you said it. Then I knew.

EDNA   You can fool yourself but you can't fool me. I'd
                  say you were about four months gone.

                      *The kettle boils. During the following
                      dialogue,* EDNA *pours water into the teapot,
                      rinses it out, pours it into the sink. She
                      then puts a teaspoonful of tea into the pot,
                      and pours hot water in. She brings some old
                      mugs to the table, along with cream and
                      sugar. Meanwhile,* MOLLY *bursts into
                      tears.*

                  Cryin' won't help. Will the boy marry you?

MOLLY   He's a Doukhobour!

EDNA   Oh Lord.

MOLLY   Come to help with the seedin'. In spring.

EDNA   Then marriage is out. Doukhobours's bad as
                  Protestants.

MOLLY   Da'll kill me.

EDNA   You've been a fool, that's certain. You want
               milk in first?

MOLLY   You got any cream?

EDNA   We got *heavy* cream.

               > MOLLY *starts to ladle sugar into her cup.*
               > *Like* HARRY, *she takes a lot.*

               You want a sugar baby? I'll get the heavy cream.
               (*goes to pantry*)

MOLLY   Oh boy, Da'll kill me.

EDNA   (*coming back with jug*) There. A spoon'll stand
               up in that. Help yourself.

               > MOLLY *helps herself, again abundantly.*

               I don't know how you kin drink it that way.

               > EDNA *sits down, pours her own tea, milk*
               > *in first, one teaspoon of sugar.*

MOLLY   How could you tell, Mrs. Delevault?

EDNA   I kin tell.

MOLLY   (*drinks tea*) Well. I guess I'll hafta kill myself.

EDNA   (*pause*) Fine idea. Don't be a stupid girl,
               suicide's a sin, and you know it, yer a good
               Catholic. If you're a bad girl, yer still a good
               Catholic. (*pause*) Let's think it out. You leave
               it to me. God works in mysterious ways.
               There's a way outa anything, if you don't let go.
               (*pause*) How old're you, Molly?

MOLLY	'n' I only did it the once! (*pause*) 15.
EDNA	Once is enough. (*pause*) All right, you have your tea then. Like a piece of pie? With heavy cream? Go good.
MOLLY	Yes please.
EDNA	All right then, you have your tea. And maybe after, I'll let you sprinkle.

Act One, Scene Three

Lights up, dim, on bedroom upstairs. MOLLY is in bed. EDNA is already asleep on the other side of the bed. MOLLY is trying to keep quiet, but now and then she sobs. HARRY stands at the door, switches on the overhead light.

HARRY	Well, now, what's this, Miss Molly Dorval? Homesick first night?
MOLLY	Oh, you gotta light in here too!
HARRY	Sure I do. See? (*turns it off, then on, off, then on*)

MOLLY laughs.

So? I don't want no measlin' girls around this place.

MOLLY	It's not that.
HARRY	First night away from home.
MOLLY	(*shakes her head*) Not that.

HARRY   Mother Delevault worked you too hard—you did fine job tonight, with supper. With washin' up. Fine job. 'n' you just see what Miz McGrane brings back with her from Calgary.

MOLLY   What?

HARRY   Mmmm mmm. Spoil surprises, tell them.

MOLLY   I'm not homesick. I like it better'n home. But I can't tell.

HARRY   (*crosses to her bed, sits on it*) Well, you tell me a story then.

MOLLY   Me tell you a story?

HARRY   Mmmm. I need a bedtime story. Tell me...best time you ever had, your whole life.

            MOLLY *laughs.*

            I'm serious, Miss Molly, I want bedtime story. (*leans back comfortably against foot of bed*)

MOLLY   Oh Mister McGrane! (*shushes him with her finger, indicating* EDNA, *who turns and mutters in her sleep*)

HARRY   I'm waitin'. Stay here 'til sunup hafta.

MOLLY   (*laughs*) Well. *You* won't think it's best time.

HARRY   You might be surprised.

MOLLY   Well. Up at my uncle's place, Charlie Fabrizeau's? Porcupine Hills? They got a hot spring. My Uncle Charlie, he's got it all wired off so's us kids won't get at it. But we do anyways. It's lovely and hot and it smells like old eggs the hen hid and then forgot where she put 'em.

> HARRY *smiles, his eyes closed.*

(*encouraged*) My Uncle Charlie, he says that's the smell a the fiery pit, that's the smell a fire 'n' brimstone and the Devil's goingta drag us down by our heels, but that's just ta scare us off.

HARRY   But you aren't scared off.

MOLLY   Naw! See, it's ony an underground river feeds that spring, deep under ground, down near the centre a the world, and it's boiling away down there and it comes up all bubbly and hot and steamy. My cousins 'n' me, we used to sneak up early mornings...(*snuggled down now; sleepily*) One time, one time we was there fer first snow, and we snuck up then too, and it was really somethin'. The snow comin' down and there we was, naked, with icicles hangin' from our hair 'n' our eyelashes, and Jack's nose had this long icicle! (*small laugh*) An' all around us, the snow was fallin' and everythin' was so quiet an' still and we was warm. Naked 'n' warm. ...I think my Uncle Charlie? He knew. I jest think he never really wanted to catch us. I think he'd done it too, he was young...(*drowsy, dropping off*) Snow fallin' down and everythin' so quiet and still and us, all warm and naked.

> HARRY *waits a moment. He gets up, goes to her and looks at her. He covers her with the quilt. He bends down, and kisses her forehead. In that moment, he knows he feels more than fatherly interest for* MOLLY. *Slight reaction, then he laughs at himself.*

HARRY   God bless, Molly.

He goes out and shuts off the light.

Act One, Scene Four

The day of JENNIE's *return.* MOLLY
*comes into the kitchen with fresh
flowers—Tiger Lilies, Brown-eyed Susans.
She puts them on the side of the sink, and
pumps water into a jam jar.* EDNA *is on
her knees with a waxing brick, giving a last
polish to the linoleum.*

EDNA   Wasting good well water?

MOLLY   Ony a bit. Fer th' flowers. (*puts jar of flowers
on the kitchen table*) There, that looks nice.
She'll like them flowers. I went all the way up
to th' Indian rings for them Tiger Lilies. (*pause*)
I'll put the kettle on.

EDNA   They won't be here for ages yet.

MOLLY   Oh no, truck just come over bridge.

EDNA   (*on her heels*) You heard truck come over bridge?

MOLLY   Just now. (*moves kettle to hot part of range*)

EDNA   Bridge's a good piece away.

MOLLY   Oh I got good ears. My da says I can hear grass
grow.

EDNA   (*speaks as if* JENNIE *were dead*) My Jennie used
to hear things. I better get away this waxing
brick then. (*gets up stiffly*) Yes, my Jennie was
like that. My Jennie could allus hear things.
(*pause*) Well, at least th' floor's done.

MOLLY   Everythin's done! My goodness, Miz McGrane's
               goingta drop dead, everythin' done and 18
               threshers fed mornin' noon 'n' night. I never
               worked so hard my whole entire life, an' nothin'
               dirty to start with!

                    EDNA *gives her a look to quell.*

               But it looks real nice, Miz Delevault. She'll like
               it.

EDNA   It needed reddin' out.

MOLLY   I think everything looks real nice. There, that's
               them comin' down the coulee now.

EDNA   I still don't hear nothin'.

MOLLY   I'll get the tea things.

EDNA   Not them old things. Jennie says use best for
               Harry.

MOLLY   Them ones in th' china cabinet?

EDNA   Yes.

MOLLY   Fer ever'day?

EDNA   It's her house. She's got her own way a doin'
               things.

MOLLY   Oh, I like them dishes. (*goes into pantry*)

EDNA   (*alone, crosses herself*) Hail Mary, full of Grace,
               the Lord is with Thee, Blessed art Thou amongst
               women, and blessed is the fruit of Thy womb,
               Jesus Christ. Holy Mary, Mother of God, pray
               for us sinners now and at the hour of our death.
               Amen. (*crosses self again*)

MOLLY   (*comes back with tray and good dishes*) Gee, they're just so pretty. I want a pattern just like this, I get married. (*pause*) Mrs. Delevault? You all right? (*sets tray on table*)

EDNA   Put on tablecloth, girl!

MOLLY   Oh!

> MOLLY *goes back into the pantry, brings back a starched, embroidered, lace-edged table cloth, and places it on the table. She then sets out the tea things.*

EDNA   You start tea then.

MOLLY   (*starts tea, kettle, etc., looks out door*) They're here then. (*pause*) Not gettin' out. (*pause*) You want I should put away the waxin' brick?

EDNA   Yes.

> MOLLY *picks up the waxing brick and can of wax, and takes them to the pantry. Just before she goes into the pantry, she pauses.*

MOLLY   I think maybe you done too much, Mrs. Delevault.

> EDNA *stands stock still and waits.* HARRY *and* JENNIE *move onto porch.* HARRY *is carrying* JENNIE's *luggage. They are moving rather slowly.* JENNIE *seems a different person—frozen, preternaturally quiet.* HARRY *scrapes his boots on the scraper and then opens the screen door for* JENNIE, *who goes to the centre of the room.*

HARRY   I'll just put these upstairs then.

EDNA   You're back then. (*pause, then to* JENNIE)
                Wipe yer shoes, I taught you better'n that.

HARRY   (*comes back in*) Too dry fer dust, Mother. Don't
                start minute she gets in door.

EDNA   (*starts to arrange teacups, etc., on table*) How's
                Mrs. Finlay?

HARRY   (*after a second's pause, when* JENNIE *does not
                answer*) Fine. Jennie says she's fine.

EDNA   And the kids?

JENNIE   (*bitter*) They're grown now. They got kids a
                their own.

HARRY   You've been turnin' things out.

MOLLY   (*comes back from pantry with ironed napkins;
                very proudly*) Yes 'n' we have too! Pantry 'n' all!
                'n' upstairs too! 'n' front room. Wait 'til you see,
                I never worked so hard my whole entire life.

JENNIE   Flowers is nice.

MOLLY   I picked them. I went all the way up to th' Indian
                rings for them Tiger Lilies.

                Everything is strained and silent.

HARRY   (*making conversation*) They're not Indian rings,
                Molly.

MOLLY   Ever'body says so, for the teepees.

HARRY   You ever seen a teepee that big around? No,
                they're old, them stones. Older'n Blackfoot or
                Peigan or Blood, older'n you, Miss Molly.

MOLLY   Who made 'em then, fairies? (*laughs*)

HARRY   Old old people. You wouldn't remember.

JENNIE   You told me they was Fire People. (*pause, then to* MOLLY) Ma shouldn't ha worked you so hard, you was just for the threshers.

HARRY   'n' she didn't fergit yer surprise, Mother. It's out in th' truck. I'll get it. Just give me half a shake. (*goes out to the porch and exits*)

JENNIE   You bin doin' too much, Ma. You shouldn't ha.

EDNA   Have some tea. (*pause*) Jennie, sit down, have a cup of tea. (*pours some milk in a cup, then pours tea*) Look, I've poured it out for you, way you like it. I've put milk in first.

                    HARRY *comes back in with a wooden crate. He sets it down on the middle of the floor, goes out to the porch again, exits.* EDNA *looks at* JENNIE, *who doesn't move.*

MOLLY   Oooooh.

HARRY   (*comes back with tire jack*) Here we are! Now, Mother, it'll be no use over ta yer sister Dora's place, 'cause Bob's so backwards lookin', but this is fer you you come here. 'course I don't expect I'll ever git a lick a work outa you again, you'll be at this mornin' noon an' night.

                    HARRY *starts to pry out the nails, causing much screeching in the terrible silence of the room.*

MOLLY   Oh what is it, Mister McGrane?

HARRY   Wait 'n' see, wait 'n' see, jeez, we got excitable

women this house, a man can't think. See, I
thought maybe we'd put it right here in th'
kitchen, over there maybe, so's everybody's got a
chance at it. (*almost manic now, talks to fill the
silence*) I thought, see, right over there, over by
that big chair, but it's up to you, Mother, it's yer
present. You say where.

EDNA   I poured you yer tea, Jennie! Sit down, sit down
        and drink yer tea!

        *There is a screech as the last nail is lifted
        out.*

HARRY   (*takes a wooden radio from the crate*) There she
        is. (*sets it down*)

MOLLY   (*awed*) A radio.

HARRY   All I gotta do is string out over there 'n' put a
        plug in an' ya kin hear London. Paris. San
        Francisco.

EDNA   Oh Harry, you got me a radio.

        JENNIE *moves to the table but does not sit
        down.*

HARRY   It was on Jennie's list, so she got it, and they
        shipped it out, same train she come on. Today.
        This mornin'. I'll fix it up tonight, you kin
        hear... Why'n't ya take off yer coat and hat, Jen?

JENNIE I don't want to. The whole house smells like a
        hospital.

HARRY   (*pause*) I guess I better get up to the north
        section, see how they've been slackin' off without
        me. (*pause*) So I'll just change my things.
        (*goes out into hallway and up to the bedroom*)

EDNA   (*calls after* HARRY) It's real nice, Harry.

HARRY   (*calling back*) But you'll never touch the knobs, *I* know!

MOLLY   *I* will! I can't wait!

EDNA   (*quietly*) You take out chicken can, Molly.

MOLLY   Yes, Miz Delevault.

> MOLLY *gets a pan from under the sink and goes out. On the porch, she looks back through the screen door, puzzled; exits. JENNIE lifts her teacup and drinks standing up.*

EDNA   Won't you sit down, Jennie, and have yer tea proper? I made pie.

JENNIE   I'll stand.

EDNA   Let me heat it up fer you then.

JENNIE   No. That was enough. I was dry.

EDNA   Let me take yer hat and coat.

JENNIE   No.

> EDNA *sits down heavily at the table. She speaks downwards as* JENNIE *stands before her. It is a confession. She cannot look at* JENNIE *until just toward the end.*

EDNA   Jennie, you got to try to understand. It was a terrible year. A bad terrible year. First yer dad died. In the spring. But I bore up, because there was you and Ben. An' I had ta bear up. You kin bear up when you got to. But then we lost the farm. It broke Ben's heart ta lose the farm. (*pause*) That's the worst thing for a farmer, to lose the land. And Ben went inta the mines. Ben was a farmer, like Harry's a farmer. Ben could stand on a piece of land, and Ben could *know*. What it was for. Oats or barley or wheat or time to summer fallow. Your dad used to say Ben could smell land through his feet. (*pause*) Like you kin hear things. My children were gifted! But then we lost the farm and Ben had ta go inta the ground. And then they come to tell me. He hated it so, down there in the dark.

> EDNA *looks up at* JENNIE, *holding out her hand for* JENNIE *to take. After a moment,* JENNIE *takes the hand.*

You and I, we waited it out then, you and I, Jennie. How long was he there, breathing and breathing and watching the light go out, then not using candles for fear a usin' up the air. It was eight days and nights before they found him, but how long did he wait, Jennie, down there in the dark. (*pause*) I wasn't in my right mind that year. And then come the winter an' I couldn't do for the Father. I couldn't. I couldn't.

JENNIE   So you sent me in yer stead.

EDNA   So I sent you in my stead.

JENNIE   It was like the whole world froze that winter. The snow come and covered the church and the rectory so we had to dig a little tunnel to go back and forth. But I kept the stove goin' in the church and the range goin' in the rectory, and the Father kept the light on the altar goin', but nobody came.

EDNA   I couldn't come to you.

JENNIE   I liked the rectory first time you took me. I love
Aunt Dora, but she keeps a cold house. But I
liked the rectory. It was like livin' in a cave.
And sometimes, when my work was done, I'd go
through the tunnel to the church and I'd pray to
the little light, and it seemed like you was there,
Ma.

EDNA   There was no way to get in or out, the whole
world was buried.

JENNIE   (*insistent*) You was there, Ma.

EDNA   Well, I never wanted to live with Dora, we never
got along. It's true she keeps a cold house.
(*pause*) Well, it's past and done with now and no
use cryin'. Jennie? Jennie? Maybe it's too soon
to say what I got to say, but, never leave off a
job needs doin', do it right away, you can't suffer,
and here it is, see, what I've thought out, like
God answered a prayer. See, the Dorvals is good
stock, Jennie, French way back like us, 'n'
Catholic, an'...the boy...well, the truth is, the
boy's a Doukhobour. So see, what I was
thinking, oh I forgot, you don't know how it
stands with Molly. She's in the family way.

> EDNA *waits, as if expecting an interruption.*
> JENNIE *has gradually, with growing horror,*
> *pulled her hand away, and moved back into*
> *the centre of the room.*

'n' you 'n' Harry, you could adopt...Molly's...
baby. (*pause*) I was prayin', prayin' for an
answer. And in comes Molly. I could see at a
glance. Four months gone if she's a day.
Anybody with an eye could see. It's a wonder her
own mother never...but a mother never sees...so
they don't even know yet. The Dorvals.

JENNIE   (*in horror*) You knew all along. That's why you
          never wanted me to go to the doctor. The doctor
          said you knew. The doctor said you signed the
          paper.

EDNA   (*denying*) I never knew what it was for!

JENNIE   It was a paper to have me cut. And you knew. I
          said to the doctor, "That's a lie, my ma'd never!"

EDNA   I never!

JENNIE   You knew. 'n' you got it all worked out, even
          'fore I got home, how I kin adopt Molly Dorval's
          bastard.

EDNA   I wasn't in my right mind!

          JENNIE *continues to stare at her. Pause.*

          I swear, Jennie, I never understood what I was
          signin'. (*knows now that she cannot convince
          JENNIE*) All right. All right. But you was in
          that place. I would've done anything to get you
          outa that place.

          JENNIE *continues to stare at her. Pause.*

          He said it was for yer own protection!

JENNIE   The doctor read it to me. He cut me to stop the
          transmission of evil. (*terrible humour*) You
          allus said God couldn't blame me fer the way I
          was made. I'm not the way God made me, Ma.
          (*small laugh*) I still can't take it in. Maybe it's
          true I'm not bright. It must be true fer people ta
          sign papers 'n' do that to me. Maybe I'm not
          bright. But I'm not the other...You were my
          mother!

EDNA   Oh dear God, blessed Jesus, he was the priest, Jennie!

JENNIE   'n' you knew that too.

> JENNIE *takes off her hat, which is attached to her coiled hair with a hat pin. She goes to the range. She lifts a lid with the lid lifter. She puts the hat in the fire, and then stares into the fire as it burns. Then she throws the hat pin in as well. She replaces the lid. HARRY comes back into the kitchen in work clothes. He has been sitting upstairs, waiting for the women to say whatever it is that has to be said.*

EDNA   (*over his entrance*) Oh Jennie, Jennie, you burnt your beautiful hat. Harry, Jennie's just burnt her hat.

JENNIE   Harry, you kin take Ma back to Dora's Bob's place now.

HARRY   (*pause*) She ain't heard the radio—

JENNIE   It's time! She's done too much.

EDNA   She burnt her new hat you bought her to Lethbridge.

HARRY   She has ta get her things together, Jennie.

JENNIE   Take her now, Harry. You kin take her things tomorra.

HARRY   (*goes to screen door, opens it*) Come on, then, Mother.

EDNA   (*starts toward door, stops, looks back at* JENNIE) Jennie.

JENNIE   Go, Ma. Please. Go. Harry, get her outa here.

                *HARRY and EDNA go out screen door. He
                puts up his hand to help her off the porch,
                and they exit. JENNIE stands stock still in
                her kitchen. MOLLY comes up on the
                porch carrying an empty chicken can, and
                goes into the kitchen.*

MOLLY   Is yer ma goin' already? Ain't she goingta stay 'n'
                hear radio? (*pause*) 'n' she never tuk her things.

JENNIE   She says yer in the family way.

MOLLY   Oh jeez, Miz McGrane, and she's never let up on
                it since I got here.

JENNIE   What's it like?

                *MOLLY doesn't quite know what to do.
                She washes out the chicken can, then later
                starts to clear the tea things away. JENNIE
                watches this girl taking over her kitchen.*

MOLLY   Well, most a the time it's not like anything. I
                don't even think about it... I ony did it the once.

JENNIE   That easy.

MOLLY   Well, it ain't so easy fer me, I kin tell you. My
                da'll kill me.

JENNIE   Stop doing that...I mean, stop rushing around.
                Sit down. (*pause*) Sit down, Molly. Here.
                You've been worked off yer feet last four days.

MOLLY   (*sits at the table*) Ooof! Have I ever! Yer ma,
                she's a slave driver.

JENNIE   Have yer tea.

MOLLY *helps herself in her usual gluttonous way.* JENNIE *sits down at the table, very carefully, as if she feels she will break.*

What's it like.

MOLLY   Well, it's sort a like...a little fish...in a underground river. Ever' so often you can feel its little tail go flip flup! (*laughs*) But most a the time I don't think about it. (*adds more cream, sugar to her tea*)

JENNIE   You don't feel sick or nothin'?

MOLLY   Me? Naw! I'm healthy's a horse. See, if I don't think about it, or I don't get this little fish tail in the river feelin', I don't worry. It just seems like any other day.

JENNIE   Yes.

MOLLY   On first night here, I thought about it. After I got inta bed. *Then* I thought about it. Oh jeez! Well, I said, it's just the end a the world, that's all. (*laughs*) Then Mister McGrane come in and turned on the light for me, and that made me feel better.

JENNIE   Harry came into your room?

MOLLY   Yeah, come in, turned on the light, said, tell *him* a bedtime story, so I did, next thing I knew, I was dead ta the world. (*laughs*)

JENNIE   Where was my mother?

MOLLY   Side me, in bed wore out, dead ta the world. (*pause*) I guess you think I'm a bad girl now though.

JENNIE   Maybe you couldn't help yourself, 'cause yer not
                too bright!

MOLLY   (*defensively*) I passed my junior matric! I got
                confirmed!

JENNIE   *I* got confirmed.

MOLLY   I am too bright!

JENNIE   People allus said I wasn't too bright.

MOLLY   You! (*laughs at the absurdity of this*)

                JENNIE *tries to normalize this new reality,*
                tries to make it seem possible.

JENNIE   Well, I never even got my grade seven. My dad
                started to get sick and I was taken outa school and
                went ta work for Mrs. Finlay up to Lumbreck.
                But I didn't mind because my teacher?... Mrs.
                Williston?...

                MOLLY *grimaces. She too has had Mrs.*
                Williston.

                She said I wasn't too bright anyways. My ma
                allus said that was the way God made me...and I
                wasn't to blame. Even...even Harry jokes me
                sometimes. He says I got brains else. I kin hear
                things. When people die. Or a car comes 'cross
                the bridge. Or someone needs me. And Harry
                allus said it never made no mind 'cause I had
                brains else, but I never got my grade seven.
                (*pause; with great pain*) I shoulda got my grade
                seven.

                MOLLY *doesn't understand what* JENNIE *is*
                saying, but she understands that something
                is terribly wrong.

I better go get changed now, the men'll be in
soon fer their supper.

MOLLY   Oh jeez.

> MOLLY *jumps up, starts to clear the table.*
> *She starts to lay out the table with plates.*
> *She checks the range, checks the vegetables.*
> *In other words, she takes over.* JENNIE *gets*
> *up and starts toward the door.*

'n' it's th' last night too! Tomorra they'll be
done. Mister McGrane's been lucky! He's got
his whole crop in and still not a cloud in the sky.
Miz McGrane? Do you think Mister McGrane's
goingta fix up that radio tonight for sure? I'd sure
like to hear that radio.

JENNIE   You ask him.

MOLLY   Ony, he should never leave it in here, Miz
McGrane. I mean, it's more a front-room-lookin'
sort a piece of furniture, isn't it?

JENNIE   Maybe.

MOLLY   Oh yes, a radio's more a front room sort a thing.
Ony, winters, you'd hafta leave stove on in there.

JENNIE   (*pause*) I'm sorry I said that, Molly, about yer
not bein' bright. I'm just a little tired.

MOLLY   Oh that's all right, Miz McGrane. I guess I was
a bit dumb, I mean, even if I did do it ony the
once. (*pause*) Why don't you go on up and lie
down fer a bit. I can handle everything down
here.

> JENNIE *looks at* MOLLY *and acknowledges*
> *this truth. She goes out into the hallway*

and we see her go into the bedroom. She stands there, a woman with nothing to do.

Act One, Scene Five

The next evening. Outside a heavy rain is falling. We can hear it, and we can see that the porch is wet. A real summer rain. Thunder. Lightning. From off, inside the house, we can faintly hear the sound of the radio in the front room, and, sometimes, MOLLY's laughter. JENNIE stands on the porch, looking out at the rain. HARRY comes onto the porch, shakes off his hat and jacket, and hangs them on pegs outside the door. He wipes his head and neck with a kerchief.

HARRY   I put milk in separator shed. (*pause*) Poor ol' Bailey, his whole quarter section got hailed out.

JENNIE   And you just done yestiddy.

HARRY   Yeah. Mine's all in. All yestiddy. I think it hit Waterson's place too. I could see that big purple cloud movin' over that way. Hunh. Molly sure likes that radio.

JENNIE   Maybe you should keep her.

HARRY   If you want. She'd be company fer you.

                Awkward pause. They haven't talked, so this is the moment for it.

                Well, men're happy anyways, all paid off, so that's done. Take wheat inta town tomorrow. Nice to have them gone though. Even when they're out there in the bunkhouse, ya know they're out there. Nice to be alone.

The radio is heard, faintly.

JENNIE   Except for Molly. (*pause*) It's clearin'.

HARRY   Yeah, them hard rains, they clear up quick. Do their damage and turn soft.

JENNIE   (*doesn't turn to look at* HARRY) I guess you want to ask me.

HARRY   Well, I guessed it wasn't good news. I figured you'd tell me you was ready. (*pause*) I don't see why you tuk against yer mother though.

JENNIE   You didn't sleep much last night.

HARRY   No more'n you, seems.

JENNIE   It's clearin'.

The rain stops. Music from the front room, faintly.

HARRY   You don't hafta tell me, you don't want to. It comes to same thing.

JENNIE   No it doesn't.

HARRY   Well, there's things, Jen, I never told you.

JENNIE   It's bin a whole day 'n' a whole night 'n' another whole day 'n' another whole night and everythin' seems just the same.

HARRY   When I was out at the Coast, I got inta trouble... I was in prison...that's why I was away so long. Why I never come home my father died.

	For funeral.
JENNIE	Prison? You was in prison?
HARRY	I told you, you'd have married me?
JENNIE	I wish you'd told me.
HARRY	You'd'a married me, I told you?
JENNIE	Yes.
HARRY	(*tries to make this a joke*) Well, then, I didn't hafta tell ya, did I?
JENNIE	Have you known about it all along?
HARRY	Jen, we don't hafta talk about it.
JENNIE	We do, oh God, Harry, I wish we didn't, but we do, we hafta talk about it. And I don't know how. I don't have words ta talk about it. You don't know, you don't know.
HARRY	I know some'v it. People said things. When I come back and you was workin' there, at the rectory. 'n' I started courtin' you. People said things. Bill Jackson said something, down at Feed Store, so I just took him out back a Feed Store 'n' talked to him a bit. I didn't touch him, I ony talked to him. I said "Spew it out, Bill Jackson, 'cause the banns're called two weeks now, and after next Sunday's bann's called, I am marryin' me Jennie Delevault in the sight a God 'n' Man, and I'll hear nothin' agin my wife that day forward."
JENNIE	Then you knew. An' Ma knew. Ony you don't know. Not all'v it. An' Ma, she had it all worked out, ta take Molly's baby. (*laughs*)

HARRY   (*not understanding*) Take Molly's baby?

JENNIE   Harry. (*pause*) That doctor cut me. All that time ago. When the Father tuk me to that place. It wasn't no regular hospital. They sat me down and asked me questions, ony I'd sworn not to say, 'n' they said I wasn't too bright. They said—they was four a them—they said I was feeble-minded. I never had no appendix.

HARRY   Were you in the family way?

JENNIE   (*shocked*) No! Oh no. No, he'd'v never done it *then*. No. Oh if I'd been late, it would've been a sign, it would've been a punishment, he'd've never gone against God like that. No. They just cut me.

HARRY   Where? What place? What hospital was it?

JENNIE   Ponoka. 'n' it wasn't just feeble-minded they said.

HARRY   (*carefully, very quiet*) Who took you?

JENNIE   See, I was 16, and so they had ta get... Ma had to sign the paper... See, Harry, when I wrote the letter to that doctor, the one who done it, he said he didn't know what to think. That's why he wrote back so fast, come up to see him in Calgary. He's in private practice now. He was just startin' out then, ony job he could get. Anyways, he said, he said, he said...he didn't have no idea I could write a word of English. (*tries to laugh, numb with shock*) See there's this law, Harry. Against "the transmission of evil." And they said I wasn't too— No, they said I was feeble-minded. 'n' the other.

HARRY   What other?

JENNIE   I was evil.

HARRY   (*almost laughs*) Who said?

JENNIE   The people in that room. Who asked me the
           questions. There was four a them, three men an'
           a lady. 'n' they asked me questions. But see, I
           swore'n oath to say nothin', 'n' I never. (*pause*)
           That's funny. Everybody knew. That's funny,
           Harry. But I never said. 'n' the doctor, he's in
           private practice now, oh I told you that already,
           the doctor said, "Mrs. McGrane, I don't know
           what to say. I didn't know you could write a
           word a English." He said I wrote him, he was
           dumbfounded. See, if someone signs a paper,
           they can cut you out. And Ma, she signed it.

HARRY   Who took her the paper? (*pause*) Who took you
           to that place?

JENNIE   (*in spite of everything, still feels she cannot
           betray her word*) The doctor said, he can't fix me
           back again, Harry. I don't seem to be able to take
           it in. I don't feel anythin'. It's like my body
           don't belong to me no more. You got your
           whole crop in, Harry. Look how clear it is.

HARRY   Who took you there? Who took yer ma the paper
           to sign?

JENNIE   Ah. He did.

HARRY   I want you to say it. Say his name.

JENNIE   See, they didn't even hafta tell me or nothin'
           because I was a minor! See how clear it is,
           Harry!

           "Look at the stars! Look, look up at the skies!
           Oh look at all the fire-folk sittin' in the air!"

	If I was feeble-minded, how could I remember the words you taught me?
HARRY	Say his name.
JENNIE	Father Edward Fabrizeau. (*pause*) There. Now I've told, and you can kill me. (*pause*) Ony when I go, Harry, don't put me in the ground, I want to go like the fire-folk, burnin', burnin', like those old Fire People made the rings up on the butte. (*laughs with the relief of it*) Take me down ta the river and cut me some kindlin', and let me go up inta the sky like fire-folk. (*laughs*)
HARRY	I'm not goingta kill you, Jennie.
JENNIE	Haven't you heard what I've bin tellin' you? You got to kill me, Harry. An' then him, you got ta kill him too. I swore I'd never tell, an' now I did, and I told him you'd kill him.
HARRY	(*pause*) I kill ya tomorra. (*pause*) Right now, you go up, get you some rest.

> JENNIE *goes into the kitchen, gets the kerosene lamp from the top of the shelf beside the sink, and lights it.*

| JENNIE | Oh! I did it again. You see what I did? I'm just not too bright, it's true, Harry. Molly, she's not ascared a bit. I don't know why, everythin' strikes me funny. Mr. Bailey gets hailed out and you don't. Luck a the Irish. (*tries to laugh, turns to hallway*) |

> *The sound of radio music, faint. Laughter.*

She'll stay up all night, listenin' ta the ends a the world.

HARRY   Go to bed now, Jennie.

JENNIE   Yes. Yes, I'm tired out. Good night, Harry.
               (*exits into hall*)

HARRY   Good night girl.

               JENNIE *enters the bedroom and places the
               lamp on the bedside table. The light on the
               bedroom dims. Now we see only* HARRY.
               HARRY *comes into the kitchen. He has
               been holding himself in. He goes to the
               range, lifts a lid, puts in more kindling,
               replaces lid.*

Oh Jesus!

               *He places his right hand down, hard, on the
               hottest part of the range.*

Act Two, Scene One

*The bedroom, two nights later. MOLLY is
finishing her tidying in the kitchen. The
bedroom is dimly lit. MOLLY takes her
apron off, looks around with satisfaction,
and goes into the front room, turning off the
light. The radio flares up, then becomes
subdued, and then silent. HARRY comes in
from outside, wiping his boots on the
scraper. He goes to turn on the light, then
doesn't. He takes off his jacket painfully.
We can see the bandage about his right hand.
He goes upstairs to the bedroom, enters,
then hesitates.*

HARRY   It's been two days you stayed in bed, Jen. It's not
good for you. (*cradles the burnt hand with his
other hand*) I know you're not sleeping. Nobody
could sleep so many hours and days away. You're
not asleep. (*turns on the light*)

JENNIE   Don't do that!

HARRY   Come downstairs, Jennie.

JENNIE   Things're gettin' done, aren't they?

HARRY   I didn't mean that.

JENNIE   She's takin' care of things, isn't she?

HARRY   Jennie, it's no use, you can't hide yourself away
from it.

> HARRY *sits on the bed.* JENNIE *moves
> away from him.*

Something bad happened to you.

JENNIE   It happened, so it happened, forget it.

HARRY   (*pause*) No, you don't forget something like that.
                But you can't brood on it. You can't just lie up
                here and brood on it.

JENNIE   I want to die.

HARRY   (*angrily*) Don't talk like that! (*pause*) Things
                happen to people. Bad things. You can't give in.
                You got to keep your hope.

JENNIE   (*turns, sits up, faces him, accusingly*) How'd you
                burn your hand, Harry?

HARRY   You're not the only one things happen to. When
                I went into that place and I heard that gate go
                clang behind me, I thought I'd never make it, all
                those years without sky or dirt or to hear the river
                or the birds... God help me, I love the world,
                Jennie. I love the world. I love it all, the way
                the thunderhead comes up all dark and purple and
                the still before it breaks, everything holding its
                breath, I love it though it'll flatten my field.

JENNIE   I hate the world.

HARRY   Don't say that!

JENNIE   I was your gift, Harry, I brought you luck. But
                he told you, the ony luck is the devil's luck.

HARRY   We can make our own luck. We can make a life.

JENNIE   How did you burn your hand, Harry.

HARRY   I know how it is, at first. Black despair. Alone
                in a cage. Some old guy there, he said, first day,
                "You can do your time easy or you can do it hard.
                But whatever way you choose, you'll do your

time." I'd'a been like you maybe, nobody got me up and out to march around the yard half hour a day. I hated that half hour at first. It was too little and too much. I wanted to go inside myself and never come out.

JENNIE   Yes.

HARRY   Jen.

JENNIE   I feel so dirty.

HARRY   (*reaches out and puts his bandaged hand on her*) Jen, come back.

JENNIE   (*grabs his bandaged hand and hurts it, so that he pulls away*) Why'd you burn your hand, Harry? So you'd never have to touch me again! That's it, i'n't, Harry, so you never have to touch me any more.

HARRY   No no no. Listen to me. Listen. Try to understand.

JENNIE   I can't understand, remember? I'm not too bright.

HARRY   It's *I* can't understand it. It's me, I can't understand how it could happen. What happened at first, it's ony nature. The Church says it's bad, but it's ony nature. But what happened after, what he did to you, I can't understand how he did that. It's even against the Church.

JENNIE   And you forgive him, you're that good a Christian, you forgive him?

HARRY   I can't understand him! I'm not God, to punish him!... I think I can't be a Christian at all sometimes, I love the world too much.

JENNIE   Oh no, you're a big Christian, you forgive him,
            you forgive me. You burnt your hand you
            wouldn't have to touch me. No... No, you burnt
            your hand you wouldn't have to kill me...

HARRY   (*takes her by the shoulders and shakes her*) Damn
            it, Jennie, you're alive and life's a miracle! The
            rest we can swallow.

JENNIE   No, no, so you wouldn't have to kill him...
            That's it, isn't it, so you wouldn't have to kill
            him!

HARRY   (*stops holding her*) I think you should come
            downstairs now, Jennie.

JENNIE   You coward.

HARRY   Come downstairs now.

JENNIE   What was you in prison for?

HARRY   ...you got to come downstairs again.

JENNIE   I could start getting up half hour a day, march
            around...

HARRY   If that's all you can manage. You can't stay up
            here forever.

JENNIE   (*pause*) All right. I'll get up like a prisoner,
            march around half hour a day. What did you do,
            Harry? What was *you* in prison for?

HARRY   I'll tell you one day.

JENNIE   Lie down beside me, Harry. I'm so cold.

            HARRY *lies down beside her.*

...I'm no good for anything.

HARRY   Shh shh.

                JENNIE puts her arms around him, then
                crawls over him, rubbing herself like an
                animal against his body. HARRY tries to
                respond but can't.

JENNIE   You see? You can't make love to me any more,
                Harry. I'm not a woman to you now.

HARRY   It's not that.

JENNIE   I was your gift. But you're cursed now, Harry.
                I'm your hoodoo. (*a long wail of pain*)

Act Two, Scene Two

                Winter, just before Christmas. HARRY sits
                in the armchair, staring out the storm door.
                The inner door is open, so he can see
                through the glassed outer door. He has a
                rifle beside him, leaning against the chair.
                A cold late blue afternoon coming on to
                evening. MOLLY comes in, dragging a
                pine tree, just chopped. She is very
                pregnant and somewhat awkward.

MOLLY   I got a tree. Fer Christmas. Thought I'd put it
                up.

HARRY   Wondered where ya got to.

MOLLY   I strung berries too, see?

                MOLLY shows him the dried berries strung
                for the tree, then starts to take off her outer

clothing—boots, coat, leggings, toque,
scarf, mittens.

Thought I'd better, before it really blows.

HARRY   Yeah, she's goingta turn tonight. Get real cold.

MOLLY   Yeah. (*turns to the sink, sees the supper tray*
untouched; disgustedly) She didn't eat nothin'
again? (*scrapes the supper plate into the chicken*
can) Well, pigs eat good here. Chickens eat
good this place! (*pause*) Ben Collette cleared
road down.

HARRY   Hunh. That's Ben Collette all over, clear road
down afore the big snow comes. (*pause*) Miss
the bridge again?

MOLLY   (*small laugh*) No, he cleared it down to the gate,
right down, he didn't hit the bridge this time. But
it's comin' all right, you kin feel it. (*shivers,*
puts kindling into stove part of the range)

HARRY   Trust Ben Collette to clear road down just before
Hell freezes over.

MOLLY   Yeah, we're goingta be snowed in all right. (*goes*
to the box of kindling beside the door)

HARRY   Don't stand in my way, Molly! I see that bastard
I might shoot you instead!

MOLLY   Oh Mister McGrane. (*sits down at the kitchen*
table and begins to pick at the wood with her
fingers)

HARRY   Oh go listen to radio, Molly. Don't pick at the
table. You picked that table inta slivers.

MOLLY   You're always after me! An' I got th' tree fer

Christmas an' everythin'! (*pause*) It's like livin' in a tomb!

HARRY   (*pause*) Sorry. Go listen to the radio, Molly.

MOLLY   I thought maybe we could decorate the tree together. I found the ornaments from last year.

HARRY   I got to watch fer that coyote. Maybe later.

MOLLY   Ony, I couldn't find the little stand, fer the tree...

HARRY   I'll get it.

MOLLY   It's drippin' there. (*indicates the tree*)

> HARRY *looks at her. She sighs, gets up, goes into the hall and exits. After a while, faintly, we hear Christmas carols, but they fade out almost immediately.* JENNIE *turns up the kerosene lamp in the bedroom. Her hair is all about her face, wild. She is in a dirty flannelette nightgown, and the buttons are undone between her breasts. She doesn't put on slippers. She takes the lamp and comes downstairs. She stands in the doorway for a moment and then puts the lamp on the side of the sink.* HARRY *is aware of her presence but does not look back at her.*

JENNIE   What's that drippin' all over my clean floor!

HARRY   It's Christmas tree. Molly brung it in.

JENNIE   Drippin' all over my clean floor.

> JENNIE *goes into the pantry and brings back a bucket, a cloth and a can of Armstrong and Hammer lye. She fills the*

> *bucket with hot water from the boiler part of the stove, and pours lye into the bucket. She dips a cloth in and wrings it out. It must be very hot and very painful, but she does not wince. She washes up and around the tree.*

Rubbish—she's always bringin' in rubbish! Rubbish. Filthy rubbish. I don't want that girl here no more, Harry. She brings in filth.

HARRY   She's a good worker.

JENNIE   I don't want that girl here. She's not clean.

HARRY   Ony tryin' ta brighten things up. Fer Christmas.

JENNIE   Whole Dorval family, it's not clean. (*stands up*) What're you readin'? (*scornfully*) 'nother poem?

HARRY   No. I'm keepin' eye out fer that coyote's been pickin' off my chickens.

JENNIE   I see the rifle, Harry. I know what the rifle's for. (*scornfully*) But I see the book too. Read me a poem, or am I too stupid to understand?

HARRY   (*takes the book from beside him, and reads*) "The world is charged with the grandeur of God. It will flame out, like shining from shook foil..."

JENNIE   That's stupid. Shining from shook foil. That don't mean nothin'. That priest wrote that too, didn't he?

HARRY   I think it's like, you know, the tin foil you get when you get a new tractor part...and you know...when you shake it off...and it shines...we got some in th' pantry, we could make a star a it, fer tree... I don't understand it myself, Jennie, I just like the sound of it.

JENNIE   (*back at the sink with the bucket, bangs the supper tray and plate*) She calls that supper? I call that pigs' slop.

HARRY   If you want I kin take her home. But I better do it now, the road's still clear.

JENNIE   That's what I want. I'm better now. I kin come back downstairs now. I kin run yer house. I kin clean yer place. I kin cook yer food. I'm bright enough fer that!

HARRY   Jennie, ever' night you come down, you say the same thing.

JENNIE   Ever' night I got to come down and clean up filth!

HARRY   Then come downstairs and take care a things yourself!

JENNIE   Why won't you kill me.

        HARRY *sighs, turns away to look out the door.*

Yer hand's better now. So kill me.

HARRY   'n' have you on my conscience too?

JENNIE   That's more important, isn't it? To be right with God. You wouldn't like ta hafta confess that, would you? That'd be a big penance, wouldn't it? That might take a whole long winter ta get through. (*laughs*)

HARRY   I think it would be better you come downstairs again.

JENNIE   (*takes the bucket up and scrubs again at the floor where the tree is still dripping*) Oh, I'll come downstairs agin. I'll do it. I can do it. I did fer Mrs. Finlay at th' United Church and she said I was th' best girl she ever had. And the Father. No one heard any complaints. Plate ledge clean. Run her finger over it, white glove 'n' all. Not a speck.

HARRY   We bin over it and over it.

JENNIE   Then shoot me. You got yer rifle. Shoot me.

HARRY   I'm waitin' fer that coyote. He's bin pickin' off my chickens. An' not just the soup hens, the layin' hens. I think it's not just a coyote. I think it's half ol' Boulanger's Sandy, half coyote. People say they can't breed, dogs and coyotes, but that damned bugger, he comes right up, he's got a layin' hen right in his teeth, squawkin'! And he gives me a grin, right 'round hen, gives me a grin just like ol' Boulanger's Sandy. Coyote's not that bold. I'd bet on it.

JENNY   Kill me and marry Molly, why not. That'd suit you. You could have yer baby then. Not *yer* baby, but a baby. A bastard's better'n nothin'.

HARRY   (*tiredly*) We could both have Molly's baby. I told you.

JENNIE   You told Molly?

HARRY   What's she goingta do, a girl 15 with a baby.

JENNIE   She's goingta sit naked ina underground river, with icicles in her eyes 'n' hair and laugh 'n' sing, though the snows come. (*laughs*)

HARRY   She told you that story, did she?

JENNIE   Yes. She told me that story. Too.

HARRY   I went to her room that night, she was scared.
                First night away from her ma. An' she'd just
                found out. She wouldn't say what it was, I just
                thought she was homesick. I never bin in her
                room since.

JENNIE   That slut's scared a nothin'.

HARRY   Ever'body's scared.

JENNIE   And Molly kin have more, after this one. And
                you like her. I kin tell. She's like a pig, a big
                fat pig. I'm not stupid, you know, I can see what
                I can see.

HARRY   That wasn't me said you were stupid!—

JENNIE   You allus said I was stupid!—

HARRY   That wasn't me!

JENNIE   I can't kill myself because you made me swear.
                All the men I ever knew made me swear. Take
                care a yer ma. Take care a Ben. Take care a
                th' farm, don't lose the farm. Be a good girl.
                Swear. Never tell. Swear. Don't kill thyself,
                swear, that's despair, that's a sin, that's the worst
                sin. (*laughs*)

HARRY   Stop it, you'll make me hate you.

JENNIE   He doesn't know, that's what I said. He doesn't
                know, I said. Because if Harry knew, he'd kill
                you. That's what I told him. Harry would kill
                you.

HARRY   He's just a man.

JENNIE   I want you to kill him.

HARRY   That's what you want.

JENNIE   Yes. That's what I want.

HARRY   That'll make us a baby.

JENNIE   Here, give it to me! (*grabs the rifle from him*)

HARRY   You do it, you do it right.   You got to cock it
                 first.   (*cocks it for her*) Then look through that
                 little "v" on the top. Don't close yer eyes, 'n'
                 hold tight to yer shoulder. No, ya got ta sight it
                 with yer eye through that little "v" an' aim fer
                 here. (*points to his heart*)

> JENNIE, *in self-disgust, pushes the rifle*
> *back at him. He takes it casually, and leans*
> *it against the chair.*

I never meant to come back to this place. This
wasn't a happy place. My old man, he was a
bully. He beat Jamie so bad, Jamie was never
right in the head. Irish temper, they said, as if it
was somethin' ta be proud of. Like luck. But it's
the prettiest place the whole river valley. 'n' th'
Indian rings. Funny. Even I call them that 'n'
know better. No, they was people livin' this
place hundreds a thousands a years ago maybe.
Before the Blackfoot, before the Peigan, before
the Blood. Older people. The ones done them
stone drawings down on Milk River. You take a
canoe and come down Milk River and you make
it a day's trip, every night fall, up on the butte,
there's Indian rings. One day's journey by canoe.
I made it three days once and every time I found
them. I always had it in mind, I'd do the whole
river. They was some kinda calendar, or almanac,
I think. Sometimes I think a them people layin'

out the stones ta tell time with. People living
here in this river valley. Lookin' up at the stars.
Waitin' out the cold. Waitin' fer the spring break-
up. Buildin' fires ta keep warm. One day I had
those damn cows a Bailey's over my side and I
goes ta drive them back, and they're there, right in
the middle a th' Indian rings. It's early on, just
afore sunup, and it's spring. It's the first day a
spring, and I'm in there, in the middle, lined up
with one a them big stones, you know how
they's four big stones placed just so, north,
south, east, west? Anyways, I'm lined up, and
the sun starts ta come up, and God! Jennie! The
sun was lined up right over that damn big stone!
I could see it comin' all around that stone, like
rays. Like hair on fire. An' the stone, big an'
black, holdin' it back, right in the centre a the
sun. It was like lookin' inta the heart a the sun.

JENNIE   Where'd they go those old people.

HARRY   (*shakes his head*) I figure it must happen four
times a year like that. I always meant to do that
too, go back, in the summer, 'n' the fall, 'n' the
deep a winter. Now. Tomorrow. (*pause*) I killed
a man once. I done it already. That's what I was
put in prison for. It's easy to kill a man. We can
make a life. We can still make a life. (*pause*) I
like it you let your hair go loose like that.

JENNIE   I got long hair. I never once cut my hair.

HARRY   First thing I ever noticed saw you in church that
Sunday. Never mind how she's braided it tight
'round her head, I says, never mind, that girl's got
lots a hair and it escapes her, no matter what.

JENNIE   I allus braided it to keep myself tidy.

HARRY   But it allus gets away on you. It's not in yer nature ta braid your hair so tight. (*pause*) Ah! There he is.

> HARRY *goes easily and quietly out to the porch, carrying the rifle. He lifts the rifle to his shoulder, fires, and waits a moment. Then he goes out to fire another shot, offstage. As* HARRY *fires,* JENNIE *holds her hands to her ears. The interval between the first and second shots is terrible for her.* HARRY *comes back up on the porch, scrapes his boots on the scraper, and comes in. He puts the rifle up on the wall, and takes off his jacket. He starts to close the door.*

's car comin' down the road.

JENNIE   I never heard it. I never heard no car. (*with wonder*) I never heard no car comin'! Harry!

HARRY   They better be quick about it, whoever, snow's comin'.

MOLLY   (*enters*) Father's car comin' down the road. It's th' Father's Dodge comin' down coulee now.

> JENNIE *turns and goes to the hallway and up to the bedroom. She does not take the lamp; she goes up in darkness.*

HARRY   Put th' kettle on fer tea, Molly.

MOLLY   You got that coyote then.

HARRY   Yeah, I'll take care of him tomorra. Got the tail anyways, they pay quarter fer the tail. Bugger, I didn't get him first time neither, and he just grinned at me. I hate it I don't get them th' first time. Had to shoot him twice ta finish it.

MOLLY   *MOLLY bustles about the kitchen, getting things ready. She goes to the door as the car pulls up.*

MOLLY   Gee, he's got Miz Delevault with him.

                              FATHER and EDNA come onto the porch. EDNA scrapes her overshoes against the scraper. HARRY opens the storm door and lets them in. He helps EDNA off with her coat, hat, gloves and scarf. She sits to take off her overshoes. She is carrying a parcel, wrapped in white tissue, which she places on the table.

FATHER   Harry.

HARRY   Father. (*does not take the proffered hand*)

EDNA   I made him bring me, Harry, afore you was snowed in. It's Christmas. I brought her a present. (*pause*) It can't go on this way, Harry.

HARRY   She's not feeling well. Molly, see if Miz McGrane kin come down fer visitors.

EDNA   Harry, I'm no visitor.

MOLLY   (*helping EDNA off with her overshoes*) Miz Delevault! The radio's workin'! I got Paris last night.

HARRY   Go up and see if Miz McGrane'll come down.

MOLLY   'n' she makes me use lye in scrub water again!

EDNA   It looks real nice, Molly. That a tree you got fer Christmas?

MOLLY   Yeah, ony Mister McGrane, he has ta find the thing ya stand it up in. (*to* HARRY) I'm goin', I'm goin'! (*goes into hall and upstairs*)

> FATHER *takes off his coat and hat. He hangs them on the back of a chair.*

EDNA   Harry, I can't stay to Dora's anymore. We had a terrible row. I'm not sayin' it's all Dora's fault, I'm not sayin' it's all my fault, but we're sisters in blood only, not by nature. Dora keeps a cold house.

MOLLY   (*knocks on bedroom door*) Miz McGrane. (*over the conversation downstairs*) Miz McGrane? Mister McGrane says will you come down, it's yer ma and the Father.

FATHER   She's got to see her mother.

HARRY   She's not got to do nothin'.

FATHER   An' you've not been to Confession neither, Harry. Not you nor Jennie, and Christmas almost here.

EDNA   She burnt her hat. I knew what it was then. She's never goin' back to the Church, I said. I knew it right then. (*pause*) I brought her a present. (*pause*) That was the hat you bought her to Lethbridge at Mademoiselle Rose's. Four dollars and fifty cents. And she put it in the fire right there.

HARRY   These things take time.

EDNA   All these months, Harry, 'n' you never come to get me.

FATHER   How will you take Communion Christmas night?

HARRY   We'll be snowed in Christmas night. Can't you smell it? You, a farmer's son?

EDNA   I bin goin' outa my mind, Harry. It's not right she should hold such bitterness against her own mother.

MOLLY   *(knocks again)* Miz McGrane?

               EDNA *starts to cry.*

FATHER   Jennie's in danger of her immortal soul, Harry.

MOLLY   Miz McGrane?

JENNIE   Tell them, yes, I'll come down.

MOLLY   Okay. *(turns, comes back downstairs, into hallway, and into kitchen)*

FATHER   In danger of her immortal soul, Harry.

HARRY   *Jennie* is!

MOLLY   She's comin'.

               JENNIE *appears behind* MOLLY. *She is wearing a new flannelette nightgown, buttoned to the neck, long sleeves. Her feet are bare, her hair is cropped off, and in her hands she holds a long fiery-red braid of hair.*

JENNIE   Merry Christmas, Mother.

EDNA   Oh Jennie.

JENNIE   'n' you've brought me somethin'! Let me see. *(takes the tissue-wrapped package and rips it open)* You don't mind I don't wait fer Christmas? Look, Harry, it's a scarf set. Look, a pretty scarf set, in white angora, with little gloves. (*puts the scarf around her neck so it hangs like a vestment*) I allus wanted one a those scarf sets.

EDNA   I made it myself, from Dora's Bob's Angora rabbits, 'fore they died off. Took me ages. Spin it right.

JENNIE   'n' I got somethin' fer you, Mother. (*lays her braid of hair in* EDNA's *lap*) Merry Christmas. I braided it first, nice 'n' tight, so it'll be easy ta carry.

MOLLY   Miz McGrane, you cut off yer hair...

JENNIE   (*going right up close*) How are you, Father? (*stares at him but speaks to* EDNA) Don't mind, Mother, it's ony what they do to nuns.

FATHER   Jennie, you got to come back to the Church. You got to forgive yer mother.

JENNIE   (*bitter, ironic*) I forgive my mother. There. All better now. I give her my hair, all braided neat and nice 'n' tight, like she taught me, to be neat, to be tidy, to be clean.

FATHER   Your heart is full a black hatred. Your mother cries all the time.

JENNIE   Do you cry all the time, Mother? Never mind. I'll take it away then.

JENNIE *takes the braid of hair from* EDNA's *lap.* EDNA *has not been able to touch it.* JENNIE *takes the braid to the stove and lifts the lid. She throws the braid into the fire and watches it burn. She replaces the lid.*

There. All gone now.

EDNA   Jennie, I swear I—

JENNIE (*turns and quells her with a look of pure fury*)
        There'll be no more swearin' in this place. I
        know what you was goingta swear. You never
        knew what it was you signed. You never
        knew. That's all right then, isn't it? If you're not too
        bright, God can't blame you. If you can't read a
        piece of paper someone brings ya ta sign, God
        can't blame you.

EDNA   Dear God, Jennie, I couldn't let you have a baby
        by *him*!

JENNIE I forgive you, Mother. I forgive you, Father.
        (*makes the sign of the cross twice*) Ego te
        absolvo a peccatis tuis, in nomine Patris et Filii
        et Spiritus Sancti. Amen. There. All better
        now.

                FATHER *crosses to* JENNIE, *spins her
                around, holds her by the arms, and shakes
                her.*

FATHER What are you doing?

JENNIE I'm forgiving you, Father.

FATHER You can't do that!

HARRY   (*moves in*) Stop that. Take your hands off her.

JENNIE (*pulls away*) Well, if I can't forgive you, Harry
        will. Let Harry go to Confession and *you* forgive
        Harry and then *Harry*'ll forgive you. Harry's a
        good Catholic. I guess that's men's business. I
        was always too stupid.

FATHER It's not Harry's business to forgive. Nor yours.

JENNIE   But he does it all the same, don't you, Harry? He
          forgives you ever'day, on his knees. Look, he
          burnt that hand to forgive you. On top of range.
          He burnt his right hand he couldn't shoot
          you...on top of range. You kin still see burn
          scar. Go on, look.

FATHER   (*not looking at* HARRY) God forgives me.

JENNIE   Well, that's God's job, i'n't it?

FATHER   I will not go down on my knees to *you*, Jennie
          Delevault!

JENNIE   Will you not.

HARRY   Jennie, fer God's sake—

JENNIE   No, Harry, not fer God's sake nor fer yours.
          Didn't you send Molly upstairs just now and get
          her to tell me, "Miz McGrane, yer mother's here
          and the Father's here and you should come
          downstairs?" Didn't you send her up just now,
          just a moment ago? Didn't you? Well, I'm
          downstairs now. It's the dead a winter now. If
          we all went out to the Indian rings and built a fire
          in the centre, and we stayed up all night, we could
          turn to the east and there it'd be, the sun behind a
          stone, lined up, lined right up. We could look
          inta the heart a the sun, isn't that right, Harry?
          We could all go out and worship when the sun
          comes up.

FATHER   You are falling into despair. That's the worst sin
          for a Catholic.

JENNIE   Despair? No. I thought it all out, Father. No,
          I'm not fallen into despair. No, it's come to me.
          That's why I cut off my hair. I got the answer
          now.

EDNA   Oh Blessed Jesus, oh Mary, Mother of God.

JENNIE   Shh, Ma, shh! I want you ta hear this. You see,
                Ma, I've got it all worked out. (*pause*) Harry can
                annul me. And I kin go be a nun. (*pause*) Harry
                can annul me, can't he, Father? I mean, the
                marriage was blessed and it couldn't *be* blessed,
                could it? I bin workin' it out. It can't be a true
                marriage the priest lies, can it.

FATHER   It was a true marriage.

JENNIE   No, if the priest lies, it can't be a true marriage.

FATHER   If the wife lies or the husband lies, it's not a true
                marriage. But a priest is a priest.

JENNIE   Ah... That's the way it works, is it. That's the
                way men work it out together. If I knew and *I*
                lied, then Harry could annul me. And if Harry
                lied, I could annul Harry. But if you know and
                you lie, and Harry finds out, he can't do nothin'
                'cause you're a priest and a priest is a priest.

FATHER   I was not in mortal sin when I married you. I had
                bin absolved.

JENNIE   You'd bin absolved.

FATHER   You must trust to God's mercy.

JENNIE   I spit on God's mercy.

EDNA   Jennie, yer talkin' crazy!

JENNIE   (*close to* FATHER *and speaking at him, though
                to* EDNA) I bin talkin' crazy since Harvest. I
                was talkin' crazy just a bit ago. With Harry. I
                was talkin', Harry, go shoot him or shoot me, 'n'
                all kinds a crazy talk, Ma, 'd bring Harry to

eternal perdition and everlastin' fire, but now I don't feel crazy. Cuttin' off my hair did it, I think. My head feels light now. I feel free 'n' I can think, and what I think is, it was an untrue blessing, and Harry can annul me. You said (*to* FATHER) God ordained the increase of mankind, and you blessed our union and called it holy. But you knew. So Harry can annul me and marry Molly Dorval. (*turns and goes to* MOLLY) Molly Dorval, may your union be holy. (*turns* MOLLY *to* EDNA) Molly Dorval, I give you to my mother who will have no more children and you kin be hers, reborn, in the fire 'n' the spirit. Amen.

FATHER   You must not speak in such a manner!

JENNIE   (*turns to* FATHER) It's true, I'm just sayin' what's true.

FATHER   I am not here to ask your forgiveness. This is between me and my blessed Lord.

JENNIE   (crosses to him) No. This is between you and me, Father.

FATHER   No. You must go to God.

JENNIE   Through you.

FATHER   Yes. Through me.

JENNIE   Ah, but I allus did, Father. I thought you *was* God!

HARRY   ...Jennie, let me take you up to bed.

JENNIE   No. Nobody'll touch me. You said, "Come downstairs," now I'm downstairs.
(*calmly to* FATHER)

You came to my bed.
I was 15.
A man of God.
And one day you took me to a place.
A place called Ponoka.
And they asked me questions there.
Four people in a room, they asked me questions.
Three men and a woman.
But you swore me to silence, and I said nothing.
And then they wrote you.
And then they sent you a letter.
And a paper to sign.
And you took that paper to my ma to sign.
And then you come back, and you said, "Jennie,
they're goingta fix your appendix and when that's
fixed, you can come home. I'll be here you wake
up." An' then they put me to sleep.
And you was, you was there I woke up.
And then you went away again.
And then you come to take me home.
And you told me, Jennie, what we've bin doin' is
a moral sin, an' we must confess to God, and we
got to stop.

FATHER   Yes.

JENNIE   I got it right then, what happened.

FATHER   Yes.

JENNIE   Sometimes I think I can't've got it right.

FATHER   That is what happened.

JENNIE   An' you lied to me.

FATHER   Yes.

JENNIE   It wasn't no appendix.

FATHER	No.
JENNIE	I got to go to God through you.
FATHER	Yes.
JENNIE	Ony here's where I think what I remember can't be true, Father. Here's where I think what I think can't be so, Father. When we got back home, to the rectory I mean, I did my confession and you gave me penance, and you absolved me. (*pause*) Then you came to my bed again. That can't be true, can it? That can not be true. Tell me I don't remember it right, Father, 'cause I'm not too bright!
FATHER	Yes. That happened.
JENNIE	Even when Harry come courtin' me. Even after that. The week before you married us. After you'd called the banns twice!
EDNA	Jennie!
HARRY	Let her finish.
FATHER	Yes. (*turns to* HARRY) I thought it would stop. I thought I wouldn't want to any more. After they did that. (*to* EDNA *and* HARRY) But at first, when I took her to Ponoka, I never meant that. It was just, to get her away! (*pause*) And then, they wrote me and they said she was feeble-minded and they did domestics often, and was she promiscuous, and if they did the operation, she could come back home, back to me, and be safe. And it seemed like an answer to a prayer. I thought it would stop the occasion of my sin.
HARRY	You did that to stop...the occasion...of your sin?

FATHER	She was like an animal! Rubbing up against me. Singin'. Allus singin'. She gave off...an odour. I couldn't get away from it, even in church! I've confessed. I've done penance. God is merciful. I confessed to Father Ogilvie before I wed you, Harry.
HARRY	They asked you, was she promiscuous?
FATHER	Yes.
HARRY	And what did you tell them?
FATHER	Well, she *was*!
HARRY	(*turns from* FATHER *in disgust*) Ah, get out of my sight.
FATHER	(*to* EDNA) I prayed to our dear Lord Jesus Christ for a miracle. The day I married them. I went into retreat, and I prayed for a miracle.

EDNA *turns away.*

God is merciful.

JENNIE	But I am not.
FATHER	(*tries to avoid looking at* JENNIE) I trust to God's Infinite Mercy. I do not despair.
JENNIE	They spayed me.
FATHER	I will not despair.
JENNIE	He does not turn His face from you.
FATHER	No. No.
JENNIE	'n' there is nothin' I could do to your God to make

Him turn His face from you. 'n' you do not
despair.

FATHER   (*frantically, to* HARRY) I despaired that winter.
That black winter. I did terrible things. Terrible
things.

> HARRY *refuses to look at* FATHER.

Sometimes, not very often, someone'd manage
to get in, and I would say Mass. I gave
Communion. I heard Confession. In mortal sin.
I despaired then.

JENNIE   That was the worst?

FATHER   For a priest it's the worst! It's not what I did to
you, Jennie Delevault, it's what I did to God!
Can't you understand?

> FATHER *is speaking directly to* JENNIE
> *now.*

JENNIE   Cuttin' me out and makin' me say it was a sin,
that wasn't the worst?

FATHER   They were terrible sins, but not the worst, no.

JENNIE   (*close to* FATHER) Why have you come for me?

FATHER   (*kneels before her*) I have come to struggle for
your soul. (*tries to pray*)

JENNIE   Get up, Father. I won't have you kneel down for
my soul. (*furiously*) No, I won't have you kneel
down to me, Father, not for my soul. Kneel
down for my body! (*presses his face against her
belly*) There, there come to me, poor Eddie.
Come to me and I will give you peace. Come to
me, poor little Eddie Fabrizeau, never could learn

to shut a cattle gate. Come to me. Come to me. Come to me.

> FATHER's *arms come up and he clasps her to him.* JENNIE *shoots a glance of fiery triumph at* HARRY. *Now she turns to the* FATHER, *and pulls his head back by the hair, so that she is speaking to him face to face.*

Damn you to Hell, Edward Fabrizeau, damn you and damn your god too, and may your soul freeze in everlastin' zero at the centre of the world. There's nothin' terrible enough I can do, is there? Except that. Not to let you have my soul. I smell, do I? Yes. Smell me now. (*pulls his head against her, and moves against him violently*) Smell me now, Edward Fabrizeau. Dead flesh. Dead woman flesh. Dead fish in a dead river. Smell me now, Edward Fabrizeau, bad man and bad priest.

> JENNIE *pushes him away from her, not violently but almost gently, and he falls sobbing to the floor.*

That's enough now.

> JENNIE *goes to the sink. She pumps water, washes her face. She picks up the water she has used before, takes a can of lye and goes into the pantry.*

HARRY (*to* FATHER) Get up. Get up an' go. Don't make me touch you. I touch you I'll kill you this time.

> FATHER *continues to sob.*

Make him stop, Mother.

EDNA
(*goes to* FATHER *but cannot touch him*) Hush, Father, hush.

FATHER
But what can I do, what can I do!

EDNA *helps him to his feet.*

(*to* HARRY) What can I do.

HARRY
You can live and do yer job an' make the best of it. Molly will have her baby and we'll take it. An' you'll do the Christenin' and you'll give the baby my name an' anoint it. You're a priest. You're a bad priest but you're our priest. So, bless this place and go.

FATHER
I can't.

HARRY
Damn you, Eddie, be a priest!

FATHER *straightens and raises his hand.* HARRY *kneels.* MOLLY *kneels.* EDNA *turns her back and does not kneel until almost the end of the prayer.*

FATHER
(*makes the sign of the cross*) Benedic, Domine, et respice de caelis super hanc conjunctionem; et sicut misisti sanctum Angelum tuum Raphael pacificum ad Tobiam et Saram, filiam Raguelis ita digneris, Domine, mittere benedictionem permaneant, in tue voluntate persistant, et in tuo amore vivant. Per Christum Domine nostrum. Amen. (*makes the sign of the cross*)

HARRY, EDNA *and then* MOLLY *cross themselves.*

HARRY
What was that?

FATHER
It's a blessing on marriage, when there's no

nuptial mass.

HARRY   (*near to tears, near to laughter*) Go on, go on, get out.

FATHER   (*puts on his coat, takes his hat*) Did the dog die?

HARRY   What?

FATHER   It was the last time I seen her, she said old Billy's dog would die. Mourn and die.

EDNA   (*realizes and wails*) Jennie!

> HARRY *turns and looks toward the pantry door and suddenly, he also knows. He races toward the pantry. Everyone stands frozen.* HARRY *returns with* JENNIE's *body in his arms. He takes her to the table, his head bent over her face, and lays her body on the table. Everyone is frozen for a moment.* EDNA *goes to the water boiler at the side of the range and begins to ladle hot water into the basin—the same basin that was used to wash Billy's body.*

HARRY   No.

EDNA   I'll wash her, Harry. I'm her mother. You get out of here now, Harry.

> HARRY *goes out onto the porch.*
> FATHER *follows him.*

FATHER   She's damned herself, Harry. She took the lye and she damned herself. I cannot bury her in consecrated gound.

> HARRY *is very still. He shivers in the cold.*

We can talk to Johnston, United Church—

HARRY   I'll take her down to the river, under the butte. I'll take her down to the river, 'n' I'll cut her some kindling. And I'll make her a pyre, like they did for the old pagans.

FATHER   You do that, they'll have the law on you.

HARRY   I'll not put you underground dark and lonely and cold. So when yer ma's made you ready, I'll burn you. 'n' I'll do it when the sun comes up. And I'll stay and watch you go like fire-folk. Into the skies.

Act Two, Scene Three

Spring. MOLLY enters with a basket. She puts it on the table. She is wearing a new dress, and her hair is loose. She peers into the basket, proud. EDNA comes in from the porch with crocuses.

EDNA   I thought they'd be nice, for the table.

MOLLY takes the crocuses and goes to the sink, pumps water into a jam jar. She puts the crocuses on the table.

Aren't ya goingta fix yer hair?

MOLLY   It's fixed, Mother Delevault.

EDNA   Yes. Yes, you look nice, Molly. (*looks into the basket, tearfully scolds* MOLLY) Now don't you go pickin' him up, he don't need pickin' up, he's sleeping.

MOLLY *looks at* EDNA, *smiles.*

Well, everythin's ready. Harry should be here any minute. I'll never forgive yer ma, her not comin' to the weddin' tomorra.

MOLLY   Oh she'll come. Never mind, she wouldn't miss it. *(pause)* They say prison changes a man.

EDNA   Not Harry. They won't beat Harry down, with their judges and their jails, and their "desecration of the dead"... *(tearfully)* We gotta put that all behind us now.

> MOLLY *comes to* EDNA *and puts her arms around her.* EDNA *almost breaks down, then steels herself.*

I'll hold Ben, fer the ceremony.

MOLLY   Yes. *(half-laugh)*

> EDNA *holds* MOLLY *close, kisses her.* HARRY *comes up on porch with a suitcase. He is dressed in a suit. He scrapes his boots automatically on the scraper, opens the screen door and comes in.*

Mister McGrane! I never heard no truck.

HARRY   I hitched a ride with Ben Collette, he let me off up at the gate. *(pauses, moves to table)* Is that him then?

MOLLY   Yes. That's Ben.

EDNA   She spoils him rotten. He doesn't get a chance to give a cry, she's unbuttoned already. If she never gives him a chance to cry, how's he goingta get lungs?

> EDNA *is very close to tears. She looks to*
> HARRY, *then to* MOLLY.

I'll take him in front room, listen to radio.
(*takes the baby in the basket to the front room*)

MOLLY (*puts the kettle on the hot part of the range*) Sit down then. I'll make some tea.

> HARRY, *bone tired, sits at his old place at*
> *the table.*

I'm sorry they wouldn't let you have yer books.

HARRY Oh, I forgot to take off my boots. (*starts to rise*)

MOLLY Oh Mister McGrane, you leave your boots on.

HARRY Those books. A man gave me those books when I was in prison before.

> MOLLY *looks at him, pulls out a chair and*
> *sits down.*

I was in prison before. I killed a man.

MOLLY (*pause*) I mem'rized somethin' you was gone, outa yer books. 'cause they wouldn't let them come through. (*pause*) You like ta hear it?

HARRY Yeah. I'd like to hear it.

MOLLY I'm a bit nervous.

HARRY (*with great effort*) Tell you what, Miss Molly, a man comes home from prison, he oughta get a piece a pie anyway.

MOLLY (*hurt, gets up*) There's pie! I was just goingta wait fer the tea!

HARRY   So, you get me a piece a yer pie, 'n' you tell me
                 yer poem. If th' poem don't give me indigestion,
                 th' pie will. And if the pie don't give me
                 indigestion, the poem will. Can't win 'em all,
                 Molly. Luck a the Irish.

                      MOLLY *realizes he's trying to joke with*
                      her. She goes to the pantry, comes back
                      with pie, plate, fork, heavy cream. She cuts
                      it and serves it to him.

MOLLY   *My* pie won't give you indigestion, Mister
                 McGrane. (*clears her throat*) The world...the
                 world...
                 The world is charged with a grandeur a God...
                 It flames out...no, it will flame out like a
                 shining of shook foil.
                 It gathers to a greatness, like the ooze a oil
                 Crushed.
                 An' all... Oh jeez, Harry, oh jeez, I fergit the
                 words. But I *know* them, just you wait...
                 Somethin' somethin'... but anyways, for alla
                 this, nature is never spent.
                 There lives the dearest freshness deep down
                 things.
                 And though the last light a the Black West went
                 Oh Morning!
                 At the brown brink eastward springs!
                 Because the Holy Ghost over the bent world
                 broods
                 With warm breast and with ah! bright wings.

                      HARRY *has not touched the pie. He raises*
                      his head now.

                 Did I do that right, Mist...Harry?

HARRY   Yeah, you did that just fine, Molly.

                      The End.

UNDER THE SKIN

Under the Skin was first produced by the New Play Centre at the Waterfront Theatre in Vancouver, B.C. in November, 1985, with the following cast:

MAGGIE Benton	*Alana Shields*
RENEE Gifford	*Wendy van Riesen*
JOHN Gifford	*Dwight McFee*

Directed by Pamela Hawthorn.
Set Designed by Paul Ford.
Stage Managed by Bill Leblanc.

The Characters

MAGGIE Benton: *An assistant professor at the nearby university. Divorced. Comfortably off. Mother of Emma. Comes from secure class, and is initially unaware of Renee's fears and envies.*

RENEE Gifford: *Pronounced Reenee. 36, thin, too made-up, too consciously feminine. Wracked with self-doubt. Sensual. Took an evening course but does not have a degree. Presently married to John. Her first husband, Nick, left her for someone younger; her children are Joanie, 9, and Dougie, 11.*

JOHN Gifford: *About 40, good-looking in a squarish way: that is, he's square-set, not fat. Wears glasses. Looks something like the Reverend Jimmy Swaggart: has some of the same physical movements and the same intense self-absorption.*

The Setting

We open on a stage that is only partly revealed. It is the kitchen of the Gifford family. It is middle class and affluent. We see it from the vantage point of the workshop, which is down the hill. We see a patio on stilts, sliding glass doors which lead into the kitchen. A door leads offstage to a hallway, and upstairs, and to the front door.

The kitchen has all the latest equipment: a microwave, a waist-high oven, matching fridge, cuisinaire set, dishwasher. The cupboards and table and chairs are wooden, and finished with verithane. There is a degree of familiar clutter—Joanie and Dougie have put up their drawings on the fridge with magnetic buttons or ladybugs. The fridge ejects ice cubes. Things are clean but just a touch off—there's a kind of embarrassing tastelessness. There are, for instance, no pottery objects, such as Maggie would have—everything has a sort of Woolworth's glaze finish. Things are a bit too bright and shiny. The canister set is labelled, for example: COFFEE, TEA, SUGAR, FLOUR, and so on. A kitchen that tries too hard but doesn't quite make it. A bit like Renee herself.

The Time

181 days, from Spring to Fall.

Scene One

*From the kitchen people can see the
sound, the greys and blues of a spring
morning, the bright thin light of a
morning of terror.*

MAGGIE   (*sits at table*) So then he said, "Well, Mrs.
Benton, we don't have unlimited
manpower." I said, "Look, I called up
yesterday and they told me she was off the
computer printout." My god, the
incompetence! I told him, I said, "Look, I
phoned yesterday and she wasn't *on* the
computer printout."

> RENEE *is making tea. She reaches up
> for cups and saucers from her built-in
> china cabinet. All the cups and saucers
> are single patterns—they don't match.
> They are displayed proudly through
> glass. There are also china knick-
> knacks in the cabinet, and a wine
> decanter in the shape of a Mexican, a
> souvenir of her honeymoon.*

You always look so—finished...in the
morning. My god, I don't think I've
showered for two days. (*smells herself*)
Shh! Yech! "She was off the computer
printout," I said.

RENEE   What did he say?

               MAGGIE *stares ahead of her. She is in
               a state of frenzy, trying to wrestle the
               world to her will. She is full of out-
               rage, furious with the police, but
               beneath the outrage and the apparent
               grasp of the situation, she is living in
               terror. Occasionally she slips into that
               terror.*

MAGGIE   He said...they didn't have unlimited
               manpower...he said they'd put her back on
               the printout.

RENEE   Well, so did you check yet to see if she's on
               it today?

MAGGIE   No. I didn't check it yet.

               RENEE *gives* MAGGIE *her tea. Goes to
               the wallphone. Listens to see if* JOHN
               *is on the phone in the workshop. Dials
               from a number written on a cute memo
               square, plastic, beside the phone. She
               checks one of the many hanging pots for
               wetness of soil as she waits.*

RENEE   Have you heard from Graham again?

MAGGIE   No. I should go home in case he calls.

RENEE   Have your tea. I think you should
               eat—Hello? Yes, this is Mrs. Gifford, Mrs.
               John Gifford? I'm a neighbour of Mrs.
               Benton's? Yes. Yes. Apparently
               yesterday's printout of missing children did
               not contain Emma's name. I just wanted to
               make sure Emma's name is on today's

	printout. Yes, yes, I'll hold. They're checking.
MAGGIE	I can't believe the incompetence. I cannot believe the sheer incompetence. (*picks up stale old toast from a plate beside her and eats it*) I said, "Who is your superior?" You know what he did? He sighed. He sighed. He said, "Look, Mrs. Benton, we don't have unlimited manpower," and he sighed as if I were boring him. (*laughs*)
RENEE	Yes? Oh it is? Okay, thank you very much. You can understand how she feels. Yes, okay, yes. Thank you. Yes I will. (*hangs up*) He said would I keep an eye on you and I said I would.
MAGGIE	And when they were looking yesterday, they were making jokes. Didn't John say that?—when they were out in the bush they were making jokes about it?
RENEE	Not about that. Just jokes. People do that. To keep up their spirits.
MAGGIE	John said though, they were laughing. (*eats another piece of toast absently*)
RENEE	Let me make you some, fresh.
MAGGIE	No, I'm not hungry, I can't eat.
RENEE	(*annoyed*) They've done all they could, Maggie. John himself has been out every day. You've got good friends.
MAGGIE	Yes, I know. (*furious*) Why shouldn't they look? If it was their kid, I'd look. I'm not

        grateful, why should I be grateful? It's
        only what's human.

RENEE   They don't even know you, you're new here.

MAGGIE   I'm human, they owe me that, they owe
        Emma that, to look. Fuck them. I've been
        here four years!

RENEE   That's new to them. —They've been out for
        a week, and she's probably just off with
        some guy she picked up with.

MAGGIE   What? Jesus Christ, Renee.

RENEE   I don't think you're in any position to take
        the name of the Lord in vain.

MAGGIE   "Some guy she picked up with"?

RENEE   You live in a dream world. Things like that
        happen.

MAGGIE   Not to people like us.

RENEE   Yes, to people like you, who says you're
        safe? Why should you be safe?

MAGGIE   We're talking about Emma, remember
        Emma? Emma with the big crush on the
        holy ghost? Emma whose big Bible was
        Anne Frank...(*hands over heart*) "I truly
        believe that everybody has some good in
        them" or crap like that while some SS was
        fucking her...Oh Jesus! No, she'd phone me,
        if she met someone and she was off with
        him she'd phone me, say she had to save
        him or some shit, she'd phone me.

Oh god. Oh god. She would have phoned me.

RENEE   You're blind about that girl. You're blind, she was asking for it. (*staring out front, towards the workshop*) The way she carries on, with John.

MAGGIE   She misses Graham.

RENEE   All right, I won't say anything. You're too upset right now. But you see, she'll phone from San Francisco, she'll ask for a ticket to fly home.

MAGGIE   I know I'm a burden to you.

RENEE   Oh god, it's been a terrible week, let me make you some food. Our nerves are all ragged. That's all. That's all it is. I had a bad night.

MAGGIE   I'll go home in a minute. I'll go home. I've got to take a shower. No, I don't want anything. Please don't make me anything. You've been good friends to me, I know I should feel grateful, I'm sorry I can't feel grateful, I think you should be good friends.

RENEE   (*staring out*) If it were Joanie I'd be mad.

MAGGIE   Yes, I thought I'd go mad at first. Isn't it funny.

RENEE   I said to Emma that time, I said, "Emma, for god's sake, you've got to use a feminine deodorant now you're menstruating because men can smell it."

MAGGIE   I've never in my life had to ask for favours.
          The police treat me as if I'm boring, a boring
          mother. I said, "Who is your superior?" and
          he sighed.

RENEE   And she should have worn a brassiere, just
          for practical reasons, your breasts start to
          sag and Emma was full-bosomed for her age.

MAGGIE   Don't do that.

RENEE   You need to eat. You've been picking at
          Joanie's leftovers.

MAGGIE   Do me a fucking favour and stop using the
          fucking past tense. Sorry. And I don't want
          eggs, for christ's sake, Renee, just let up on
          me, I don't wear a brassiere either, for
          christ's sake.

RENEE   You're swearing all the time now.

MAGGIE   I know. It's an alternative to screaming
          continuously.

RENEE   You were into a symbiotic relationship.

MAGGIE   (*laughs*) What's symbiosis anyway, I
          thought it was something to do with moss.

RENEE   Symbiosis is when you get so dependent on
          someone you can't live without them.

MAGGIE   I thought it had something to do with
          fungus. I thought the fungus lived off the
          tree and the tree got something from the
          fungus, and they were both better off.

RENEE   What would a tree get from a fungus?

MAGGIE   He sighed. He just gave this big sigh as if I were phoning about someone's dog peeing on my lawn.

        RENEE has been boiling an egg and toasting bread. Getting it ready, cutting the toast into strips.

RENEE   John says he'd bet anything that Emma's just gone off with some guy.

MAGGIE   (*as* RENEE *serves it to her*) Why do you keep saying that? Emma's never in her life done anything remotely like that. My mother made egg toast that way. (*begins to eat hungrily*) I know I'm horrible, I know I'm ungrateful, I can't stand myself either. Yeah, Mom made them just like this, I'm glad she's dead, she'd die. (*laughs*) It'd kill her. (*laughs*) I didn't even want an egg.

RENEE   You may not have noticed, but Emma's growing up.

MAGGIE   She's only 12...

RENEE   She'll be 13 on Wednesday.

MAGGIE   (*overcome with terror, clutches herself*) Oh my god, oh my god.

        RENEE comes over to hug her.

No, don't touch me, I can't stand it if anyone touches me, I'll go to pieces, don't.

        RENEE, behind MAGGIE, draws back in disgust.

She's dead. She's dead.

RENEE   Don't be silly.

MAGGIE   That's what he said to me, that officer, "Mrs. Benton, you must prepare yourself for the worst." (*laughs*) How the fuck do you prepare yourself for the worst. I can't bear it.

RENEE   You've made that girl too much in your life.

               MAGGIE *is breathing hard.*

Children leave us all some day.

MAGGIE   Not like this they don't.

RENEE   Well, at least you've eaten something. (*takes plate away from* MAGGIE)

MAGGIE   I didn't even think I was hungry.

RENEE   Sometimes I think it'll be nice when the kids go and John 'n' I are alone. John 'n' me, I mean.

MAGGIE   (*absently*) No, you were right the first time, it's *John and I.*

RENEE   Last time you said it was *John and me.*

MAGGIE   That's 'cause it was in the objective case, you said something something with John and I, and that should be *John and me.* A lot of people do that, they get upset about their fucking usage and over-correct, like saying *I feel badly.*

RENEE   I thought that was right, *I feel badly.*

MAGGIE   No, it's *I feel bad.* Who gives a shit.

RENEE   Well I do, I don't want to sound like an illiterate.

MAGGIE   Christ, even my chairman says *I feel badly.*
          "Maggie, I can't tell you how badly I feel."

RENEE   (*putting dishes in washer*) Did I tell you how
          Dougie busted in on us last Sunday morning?
          (*laughs*) God! I was sure I'd hooked the door. I
          have this routine, go to the bathroom, put in my
          diaphragm, hook the door...

MAGGIE   They said she was on the computer printout, eh?

RENEE   I told you.

MAGGIE   I better go, Graham could phone.

RENEE   You'll have to go back to work, it's no use just
          waiting around the house, it's better to have a
          routine, it gives you something to hold on to.

MAGGIE   I know people have been good, I am grateful.
          (*tearful*) People have been really good. It's just
          the police seem so blasé...I said to that young
          one, the one who came the first night, "You
          never think this sort of thing will happen to
          you," and he just looked away as if I'd said
          something...disgusting. That's the thing, they
          make you feel so disgusting.

RENEE   When Nick and I broke up, Nick and me, I said,
          No way the kids're gointa be my life, I went out
          with John three months before I ever told him I
          had kids.

MAGGIE   (*flaring*) Why should I be made to feel
          disgusting! Fuck them!

RENEE   You better hold it down when John comes in, he
               can't stand a woman with a mouth, we'd go to his
               place, and I'd say I had to be home because all my
               stuff for work was there, in a way though it
               worked out, he got really jealous, thought I was
               married and had to get back to my old man.
               (*laughs*)

                    MAGGIE *sits and stares.*

               Well, I've been lucky I guess.

MAGGIE   Sometimes I think just come and tell me she's
               dead. That way I know she's not suffering.

RENEE   Why do you keep on about that? Why should she
               be suffering? Kids run away...it's common
               knowledge kids run away with men...time means
               nothing to them...she's off with some guy...she
               isn't even thinking of you.

                    JOHN *Gifford comes in through sliding
                    doors. Goes to* MAGGIE, *embraces her.*
                    MAGGIE *starts to cry. Holds onto his arm
                    awkwardly.*

JOHN   There there. There there. We're doing all we can.

                    RENEE *looks on impassively.*

               She'll be found, she'll be found, Maggie, I know
               it. I feel it.

RENEE   (*neutral voice*) I've got your breakfast ready, it's
               in the oven. Juice?

                    JOHN, *hugging* MAGGIE, *rocks her back
                    and forth, kisses her hair.* MAGGIE, *head
                    thrown back, gives herself to this comfort.*
                    JOHN *looks down at* MAGGIE's *thrown-*

> *back face. Moment of stillness. He bends down and kisses her full on the lips.*
>
> RENEE *turns abruptly and opens oven door. Puts on mitt. Reaches in for plate of pancakes and bacon. Places them on the table.* JOHN *now moves toward* RENEE *to kiss her on the lips.* RENEE *avoids him. Goes to fridge for juice.* JOHN *pulls her around firmly, smiles at her, kisses her on the lips.*

JOHN   Good morning, Renee.

RENEE   (*looks at him*) Little early for it, isn't it?

JOHN   Hmmm. Think so?

RENEE   What's gotten into *you*?

JOHN   What's gotten into *you*—lately? (*laughs; starts to eat with appetite*) I picked up the Fraser kids this morning. Hitch-hiking. Not a care in the world. Right out there. I stopped the van and told them to get in...I said, "You kids haven't heard about Emma Benton?" They won't hitch again in a hurry. Pass the syrup, would you?

RENEE   Oh those Fraser kids, they do what they want irregardless. I've told Joanie not to bring the girl over here anymore. Who needs it.

> JOHN *stares at the cupboard under the sink which* RENEE *has opened to get some cleanser.*

JOHN   When are you going to clean that cupboard under the sink? God it bothers me...all that crud...you are really a scumbag housekeeper, Renee...my mother used to say, Look in a woman's cupboards if you want to know how she keeps herself.

RENEE Oh your mother—

JOHN Keep off my mother. (*mild*) Any coffee?

RENEE (*pouring coffee*) Her cupboards are clean, oh yes, compensation...

JOHN Quit that phony baloney crap. It's *regardless*.

RENEE Pure compensation, over-compensation...

JOHN My mother was a clean woman.

RENEE Well, she's not so clean now.

JOHN It's *regardless* not *irregardless*, ask the college professor here.

RENEE (*sing-songy*) She's rotten...rotten...she is rotten...and the worms are crawling in her eyes...

   MAGGIE *gives a high laugh.*

Sorry.

JOHN You're sick.

RENEE Sorry, Maggie, I didn't think...

MAGGIE I should go.

JOHN Give her a brandy.

   RENEE *goes toward the liquor cupboard.*

MAGGIE I should be home in case the police call. And Graham said he'd call.

RENEE *pours the brandy into an ordinary glass, puts it in front of* MAGGIE.

No, if I drink I won't be any good for the rest of the day.

JOHN

Maggie? I'm going to say something for your own good. —Drink up. (*waits until she raises the glass to her lips*) Go back to work.

MAGGIE

I can't.

JOHN

You can.

MAGGIE

No. You don't know. They're so beautiful. You walk into a lecture room and there they are, so young and so beautiful and so full of life. All that joy. All that life.

RENEE

All the sex. 18-year-olds are nothing but walking bags of hormones.

MAGGIE

Yes. All that, yes, sensuality, that sheer joy at being alive and being able to move and laugh and sing. (*drinks*) I look at them sometimes and their sheer...beauty overwhelms me. The skin, pimples and all...it just radiates. Sometimes I come out of a lecture so high...just on them, the way they are. And every year they stay the same age and only I get older. I would see them all go up in flames in the fiery furnace, just to have her back. I would see them torn to pieces. I would see the world go mad. I would bring down the sky.

RENEE

You think I wouldn't. For Joanie and Dougie? You think I don't love them like that?

MAGGIE

I could kill.

RENEE

She's just off with some hulk. You didn't see her, she was always rubbing up against John.

JOHN

Keep your mouth off Emma. I'm telling you. (*to* MAGGIE) We're all just upset and worried.

MAGGIE

(*gets up*) Thank god for good friends, I do really ...I mean to feel grateful...I will...it's just right now...

JOHN

'sallright, no need to say a word. Anytime, Maggie, I'm here. (*walks her to sliding doors, arm around her shoulder*) Try to get some rest. And think about it, going back, work's the only salvation, it's an old clinker but it's true.

MAGGIE

Yes. (*comes through the doors, onto patio, walks down steps; exits*)

> JOHN *watches her go. His gaze rests on the workshop. Turns and goes back into kitchen.*

JOHN

Joanie's been mucking about with my things again, will you tell her to leave my stuff alone.

RENEE

She only borrowed a hammer.

JOHN

She put it back in the wrong place. I have everything exactly where I want it, everything has a place...

RENEE

Just to put a poster up, in her room.

JOHN

Are you listening to me? I don't think you're listening to me. I don't care what Joanie wanted the hammer for. She could have crucified the next door neighbour's cat for all I care. Does that penetrate your brain at all? I don't care what the hammer was used for. I do not like your brat using my things.

RENEE   Oh my, what a gruffy bear this morning. What a
           gruffy bear. Ooooh oh, he has the grumps this
           morning, he has, he has, oh my what a big
           EEyore bear this morning.

JOHN   (*looking out the sliding doors*) You know
           what she said one day? (*short laugh*) She said,
           "My mom's going to take me to get birth control
           when I'm sexually active." (*laughs*)

RENEE   What?

JOHN   Are you deaf?

RENEE   Who said that.

JOHN   Emma.

RENEE   —Maggie was asking for trouble. That's all.
           Just asking for it.

JOHN   "Sexually active"!

RENEE   Maggie was always too free with that girl.

JOHN   Why don't you shut up.

RENEE   Grumpy bear this morning, grumpy bear.

JOHN   Just keep your brats out of my workshop. —Oh
           yes, she said that, for all her big religious talk.
           "My mom's going to take me to get birth control
           when I'm sexually active." I said to her, Emma,
           you've got a big surprise waiting for you, the
           world isn't like that, everybody nice and good, the
           world is just waiting for people like you,
           everybody's out for number one.

RENEE   Oh kids get religious at that age. I wanted to be a nun when I was 13—

JOHN   I don't want to hear about how you wanted to be a nun. I've heard that story a thousand times. That is completely irrelevant. What are you trying to prove? Can't you keep your mind on the subject for two minutes?

RENEE   I was only saying that kids're often religious at that age, Emma was no different, it was just a phase…

JOHN   And you keep your mouth off Emma. Do you hear me? You keep your filthy mouth off Emma. She's not like you, you're a born whore, do you hear me? Renee? Do you hear me? —Do you understand me? Renee?

RENEE   Yes.

> *JOHN stares at her. RENEE turns and starts to put dishes in the washer. JOHN gets up, moves toward her, stands behind her.*

I've got work to do.

> *JOHN pulls up her skirt and moves in to her, pushing her down over the washer.*

> *Go to black.*

Scene Two

The darkened kitchen. Late spring.

A figure against the sliding doors, pounds on the jamb. —The figure pounds again.

MAGGIE   (*calls*) Renee? Renee? Renee!

                RENEE *appears as a silhouette in the*
                kitchen doorway, turns on the patio lights,
                recognizes—after a brief hesitation—
                MAGGIE. *Goes to the sliding doors and*
                opens them.

RENEE   What is it, what's happened?

MAGGIE   I heard her.

RENEE   What?

MAGGIE   I heard her, heard her crying out to me. I heard
                her calling me. "Momma, Momma."
                Somebody's hurting her.

RENEE   It was a dream.

MAGGIE   No. I wasn't asleep.

RENEE   You were asleep.

                MAGGIE *sits down at the table. She is*
                disheveled, in an old robe.

                I'll get you a drink. (*does so*)

MAGGIE   I heard her.

RENEE   It was only a dream. (*stares out at the workshop*)

MAGGIE   It was real, I could hear her. (*shaking*)

                RENEE *gives her the drink.*

                (*holding it*) —Today one of my students came to
                see me. She wanted to complain against one of
                my T.A.'s. He's not marking the essays. He's

	just giving grades. No comments. I said I'd mark it. —That's the son of a bitch who faked his footnotes. (*brief laugh*)
RENEE	It's good you're back at work.
MAGGIE	Other people's children. I hate them. (*drinks*) I hate them for being alive and well.
RENEE	No, it's good for you to be back at work.
MAGGIE	People keep saying that to me. It's good I'm back at work. Whatshisname across the hall, he said, "You must have a steel trap for a mind." (*laughs*)
RENEE	You've got to think of yourself.
MAGGIE	Why is that.

RENEE *sighs.*

(*gulps the drink, looks at* RENEE) Such a sigh. Why such a sigh? Am I disturbing you?

| RENEE | Well, you make me...well, impatient. It's been two months. |
| MAGGIE | God yes, it's been two months, at least! I should be well over it by now. |

RENEE *sighs.*

(*puts down her drink; gets up*) Yes. You're right. It's boring. I should be able to handle it myself. (*starts for the sliding doors*)

| RENEE | No. Don't go. |
| MAGGIE | (*pauses*) Were you asleep? |

RENEE   No. —No.

MAGGIE   Everything's so clean. For once in my life the house is completely organized. No mess at all.

RENEE   Life goes on.

MAGGIE   I feel I should be screaming down the street. I feel I should be tearing the world apart. The cherry blossoms're out. Everything's alive. I should pass and the grass should wither. (*laughs*) Everything hurts my eyes.

RENEE   Life goes on.

MAGGIE   (*laughs*) That's what's so unfair.

RENEE   I've never been one to brood. When Nick and I broke up, I said, That's that, and I let him go. I went out and I met new men and I met John and I said Nick's over and done with. I opened my fingers and I let him go. I've shed enough tears for that bastard, I said. —You're young, you're still attractive.

MAGGIE   Who are we talking about, what are we talking about, a child isn't a man, you can always get another *man*.

RENEE   You've had an education. You're independent. I never had the opportunities you've had, if something happened to John we'd be done for...

MAGGIE   Oh Renee, it's not the same—

RENEE   What do you know about it? What the...christly hell...do you know about it. You've never had to struggle.

MAGGIE   I'd take a child over a man anytime, a man you

can get anywhere, a child is...a child...you give birth to a child...what the fuck are we talking about...I put myself through university, it wasn't any free ride let me tell you...

RENEE   ...you've had it all given to you, how much did that chesterfield cost? and you didn't even think twice, you didn't even wait till the sales...you just bought it...saw it and bought it...you saw it and you wanted it...do you know how long it took me to get a kitchen like this? I was raped once you know.

MAGGIE   You never told me that.

RENEE   I don't tell you everything.

MAGGIE   What did you do about it?

RENEE   What could I do? I'd known him, we'd been to bed together, Nick was working nightshift then, and I started this thing with David. Then we broke up. One night he came to our place and he beat me up and raped me. I didn't dare scream because of the baby. That was Dougie. I was afraid to tell Nick. I couldn't tell Nick, how could I tell Nick? He'd have said I let him in on purpose. Well, I did let him in, he knocked on the door and I thought, Oh, it's just David and I let him in, you wouldn't think to look at him...I didn't get my period for three months, I was terrified I was pregnant. If I was pregnant I'd have had to tell Nick, he'd have had to sign the form, wouldn't he? And then I'd have had to tell him and he'd say I let David in, I asked for it.

MAGGIE   It's a nightmare. The whole world is a nightmare.

RENEE   But life goes on, you forget.

MAGGIE   Life goes on and on and on, and it has no business going on. —I could hear her crying out for me. Sometimes I think my ears are just dead to the sounds in the air. That the air, the real air, is alive with screams of pain and terror. The abattoir across the inlet. The screams of dying fish on hooks. All the suffering of the forest. And the deep deep sea. And that what I do, what we all do, is learn to close our ears to the real noise of the night.

RENEE   Shut up.

> MAGGIE *looks at her, astonished.*

Just—shut—up.

MAGGIE   What is it? Renee? What is it?

> MAGGIE *gets up slowly. Holding her breath, crosses to* RENEE. *Takes her by the shoulders and shakes her once.*

What is it?

RENEE   —She's dead. Emma's dead. Face it. Emma's dead.

> MAGGIE *stares at* RENEE *and then howls.* RENEE *caught by her pain and by real affection and empathy, clasps her and rocks her, crying as well, rocking back and forth.*

I know, I know, oh god, oh dear god, it's not true. It's not true.

> JOHN *enters through the sliding doors. He stands there, his back to us. The women look at him.*
>
> *Go to black.*

Scene Three

*Mid-summer. On the patio. Deck chairs,
table, umbrella shade, flowers in baskets and
pots. MAGGIE and RENEE in summer
clothes, drinking tall drinks. RENEE looks
very good in shorts and top. MAGGIE is
slumped in rumpled jeans and t-shirt. JOHN
comes up from the garden, bare to the waist,
in jeans.*

JOHN   Whew! (*takes drink from RENEE and downs it*)

RENEE   (*arch*) Oh my, what a greedy bear, oh there he
goes, stealing my honey! (*laughs at him*)

JOHN   Get me a drink.

RENEE   Oh no please...no please today...oh he hates to
do the garden...he hates the sunshine...he hates
nature...what a gruffy bear...

JOHN   Get me a drink, Renee, do I have to send you a
telegram? —Can you get it through your head I
might be thirsty?

RENEE   My lord and master. Yes, sire. You command
and I obey.

                  *She gets up and archly wiggles herself in
slave-like obeisance in front of him. Raises
her hands and palms them prayerfully.*

JOHN   Move! (*pulls up chair and sits down*)

RENEE   —God, sometimes I could kill you. (*goes into
kitchen through sliding doors*)

                  *JOHN looks at MAGGIE. MAGGIE stares
ahead of her. Drinks.*

JOHN   You look like shit, Maggie. —I'm telling you for
            your own good. You look like shit. Fix
            yourself up, for chrissake. —When you going
            back to work.

MAGGIE   It's my research semester.

JOHN   So do some research.

MAGGIE   Get off my back, John.

JOHN   Forget it, forget her. She's off with some
            asshole, she's having the time of her life, she's
            not thinking about you, you'll get a phone call
            from Timbuctoo, bail me out, Mom...

MAGGIE   No. Not Emma. She wasn't like that.

JOHN   She was like that. She was like that. She was
            always out in the workshop, rubbing up against
            me. Oh it's natural, I guess, and she missed her
            dad. But she was asking for it, rubbing up
            against me. You know what she said one day,
            she said, "My mom's going to get me birth
            control pills when I'm sexually active." Sexually
            active!

MAGGIE   You think that was wrong.

JOHN   Was that true then? Did you actually say
            something like that? To a 12-year-old? Boy.
            Maggie. Shit.

MAGGIE   What're you going to tell Joanie?

JOHN   Joanie? What have I got to do with Joanie?
            —She's not my kid. That's Renee's business.

MAGGIE   She's your kid now.

JOHN   (*suddenly enraged*) Joanie has nothing to do with
             me. I am nothing to her. We're not related.

MAGGIE   I'm sorry, I didn't mean anything.

JOHN   I didn't even know she *had* kids. Asked her to
             marry me, and then I find out. Shit.

MAGGIE   Well, you're her stepfather now.

JOHN   I never bargained for her brats. She pulled a fast
             one on me there.

RENEE   (*comes out with a drink for* JOHN) There you are
             oh Lord and Master. I told Maggie she has to get
             out of the house, all she does is sit and watch
             TV. (*sits down and drinks*) That's all I *can* do as
             a matter of fact. Can you believe it, Maggie, this
             old cheapskate won't even fix our TV. I've been
             after him for three weeks now. All it needs is for
             him to take it into Jenkins', but will he make the
             effort...noooooh. (*drinks*)

JOHN   It's summer, what d'ya need TV for in the
             summer?

RENEE   Well, *I* like it at nights, when you're working.

JOHN   I've had the cable turned off anyway.

RENEE   You've what? You've what, John?

JOHN   The TV's busted, I had them turn off the cable for
             the summer.

RENEE   Aw John, aw John, aw...I *like* my TV.

JOHN   You like your fuckin' soaps.

RENEE   Oh what a gruffy bear he is this morning, oh my what a gruffy bear!

JOHN   Listen, I want you to tell Dougie to keep outa the
            workshop.

RENEE   Oh my, what a gruffy bear, what's the poor kid
            done now?

JOHN   He's been messing with my paint.

RENEE   Well, he was doing this sign for the circus. (*to*
            MAGGIE) You know, the kids're so cute, they
            got this circus going and Dougie was supposed to
            be the clown and he wanted to make this sign...a
            dime to get in...

JOHN   He moved my things. I have a place for
            everything and everything has a place.

RENEE   And Susie, from across the road? She's supposed
            to be the trapeze artist...

JOHN   Just keep your brats outa my workshop. Do you
            hear me, cunt?

RENEE   (*looks at* MAGGIE *quickly, laughs uneasily*)
            There's no need to talk to me like that. Not in
            front of Maggie.

JOHN   Maggie knows you're a cunt. Listen, Maggie?
            You know the other day, when you were talking
            to the police again? (*laughs*) And you said we
            live in the *cul de sac* off the highway? You know
            what Renee did after you left? She looked it up
            in the dictionary, only she didn't know how to
            spell it.

RENEE   I was telling Maggie, she'll turn up...she's just
            off with some guy...if it was anything else, we'd
            have heard. No news is good news, you've got to

keep hoping.

MAGGIE   Emma wasn't like that.

RENEE   Mothers're the last ones, Maggie, she was always
                at John, rubbing up against him, wasn't she,
                John, you tell her...

MAGGIE   She was on this big religious kick. She was
                always quoting those last lines from Anne Frank
                at me, what are they...oh jesus..."because in
                spite of everything...I still believe...(*choking*)
                ...that fucking people are really good at heart."

JOHN   Yeah but those aren't the last lines in the book.

MAGGIE   Yes, the last lines in that book, she was a little
                girl who hid out from the Nazis, in Holland, only
                they found her, and she kept this diary...

JOHN   I know the book you're talking about, Maggie,
                just because I'm married to a cunt doesn't mean
                I'm a cunt. I know the book and I'm telling you,
                those aren't the last lines in the book.

MAGGIE   Well, they're the last lines in the movie or
                something. Who gives a shit.

RENEE   I was on a religious kick when I was that
                age...it's sublimation...

JOHN   It's what?

RENEE   Sublimation.

JOHN   What's sublimation?

RENEE   Oh John, you know what sublimation is.
                (*laughs and looks at* MAGGIE)

JOHN   No I'm just an ignorant guy, Renee, I never went
                to no college course in psychology at night
                school.

RENEE   Well, sublimation is when you put your sex into
                something else...

JOHN   Oh, is *that* what that is. (*throws a glance at*
                MAGGIE)

                MAGGIE *smiles weakly.*

RENEE   Oh John, don't be such a bully...

JOHN   Me? I'm just trying to get an education, you
                know what it's like, living down the street from a
                college professor, I mean she just about pukes
                when she hears you going on sometimes, Renee,
                don't you know that?

MAGGIE   That's not true, John...

JOHN   She's laughing at you, for chrissake, Renee, don't
                you know that, you cunt?

                Silence.

                MAGGIE *starts to get up.*

                (*pulling her down, roughly*) Sit. Sit. Jesus.
                It's hot, it's just the heat and if it's not the heat
                it's the humidity. (*laughs*)

                RENEE *and* MAGGIE *do not laugh.*

MAGGIE   I'm not laughing at her.

JOHN   She makes you throw up, Maggie. She makes
                me throw up.

RENEE *gets up abruptly and goes inside.*
MAGGIE *twirls her glass around. Reaches*
into her pocket and takes out a cigarette
package.

You want to kill yourself?

MAGGIE   Why do you do that? Why do you talk to her
like that.

JOHN   She's illiterate.

MAGGIE   Oh for crying out loud. *(lights up)*

JOHN   You want cancer?

MAGGIE   What're you trying for, John, the Archie Bunker-
lookalike prize?

JOHN   That's how you see me, isn't it, a redneck bastard.

MAGGIE   You're the one with the hangup about class,
John.

JOHN   Oh yeah? Listen, I see you, every time she drops
some clanger, you wince, I see it.

MAGGIE   No you don't.

JOHN   I see you. When you first moved in, I saw you,
this big polite act...

MAGGIE   Renee's my friend, she's been good to me, if it
hadn't been for Renee these last months I would
have gone insane.

JOHN   You looked at us like we were bugs...you looked
at those plaques Renee's got in the kitchen like
they was shit...

MAGGIE   They're just not my kind of thing.

JOHN   Oh. "Not your kind of thing," eh?

MAGGIE   No. People have different tastes, John.

JOHN   Your kind of thing is some old pot made by some
                hippie down in White Rock. Right?

MAGGIE   Right.

JOHN   You don't like me much, do you? Truth now,
                Maggie. Truth time.

MAGGIE   (*drinks, looks at him, smokes*) No.

JOHN   (*laughs*) But I turn you on, don't I?

MAGGIE   Yes.

JOHN   Yes. But you hate my guts.

MAGGIE   You're not important enough to hate, John. I
                merely despise your type.

JOHN   My type eh? What type is that, Maggie?

MAGGIE   Renee said it. The bully. The little bully. You
                push her around because she's helpless and can't
                do anything about it. You push her around but if
                anybody stands up to you you back down.

JOHN   You think I'd back down to you?

MAGGIE   I know it.

JOHN   (*long pause*) Fuck you, Maggie.

MAGGIE   Don't you wish, buster.

RENEE   (*comes out, all made up; brightly*) Listen, I've
         put some spare ribs on, let's all have spare ribs,
         never mind him, Maggie, he's such a gruffy bear
         when he hasn't had what he wants, you know...it
         was Dougie's fault, wasn't it, John? Dougie
         burst in this morning, I'd forgot the lock on the
         door, and Dougie bursts in this morning, you
         should have seen this gruffy bear...(*looks at*
         JOHN *and tentatively sits on his knee*)

JOHN   (*sits for a moment then shoves her off*) Get off
         me, you whore. (*gets up*) I'm going to the shop.
         (*stalks off*)

         RENEE *looks after him, eyes wild.*

         Go to black.

         Scene Four
_____

         The fall. MAGGIE *and* RENEE *in the
         kitchen.* MAGGIE *is wearing a new outfit:
         pants, top, boots. She has had her hair
         done. She smokes.* RENEE *looks drawn and
         haggard.*

MAGGIE   And the chairman says he could understand that I
         was upset. Upset! I say, "Look, Benny, I've got
         an 18 page paper here, 17 1/2 pages of which are
         copied word for word from a book!" And Benny
         says I'm vindictive. He says, "However, I can
         understand what you are feeling." I said, "Look,
         Benny, this has nothing to do with Emma. This
         has nothing to do with the fact that Emma is still
         missing. That's irrelevant. This has to do with
         a simple case of fucking plagiarism. This
         fucking student has fucking well plagiarized her
         term paper, in a fourth year course, in

Shakespeare..." "She didn't even copy from a good critic," he says. Thought that would make me laugh. Then he suggests I see a good doctor.

RENEE   What're they going to do about the student?

MAGGIE   Oh, I'm contracted to lecture to her. If Miss Shitface turns up on Monday, under the terms of my contract, I must lecture to her. "Listen," I told Benny, "If that bitch turns up in my class on Monday, I will puke all over her, direct from the podium." —Then he says, "She's built like a brick shithouse." That's what he said —"built like a brick shithouse." The chairman of the English department! That's the sort of simile he uses for a woman.

RENEE   Maybe you shouldn't have expelled her from the class. Maybe that was a bit harsh.

MAGGIE   Harsh! Harsh! I'd like to string her up from her tits. How's about a drink, Renee?

RENEE   Oh yeah, sure. (*turns and gets bottle, etc. from cupboard*)

MAGGIE   You okay?

RENEE   Sure. Fine. Why?

MAGGIE   I don't know. You on a new diet again?

RENEE   No.

MAGGIE   No, people get away with everything these days, they're not wicked, they're just suffering from social maladjustment. Benny said something like that, he said the woman was emotionally disabled or something.

RENEE	Well, maybe she was! (*hands her a drink*)
MAGGIE	(*half-laugh*) Whaaat?
RENEE	You don't know why she did it. You don't *know*.
MAGGIE	I know. She wanted a good grade so she cheated. She thought it was worth the risk.
RENEE	Maybe it's not so simple, Maggie, maybe she was desperate. Maybe she couldn't write her essay and got desperate.
MAGGIE	Tough shit.
RENEE	Well, how would you know! You can always write whenever you want, maybe she needs your compassion...
MAGGIE	Maybe she needs my boot in her butt. I said to Benny, "What has her being built like a brick shithouse got to do with anything?" And he kept calling her a girl. "The *girl* has emotional problems," he kept saying. I looked her up, she's twenty-fucking-eight.
RENEE	Well, maybe she does have emotional problems.
MAGGIE	You think that excuses her?
RENEE	Well, sometimes people don't always understand the things they get caught up in, and they just, you know, get caught up in them, and they just do it, they don't work it out, like, ahead of time, they just find themselves sort of in the middle of it.
MAGGIE	I don't know, it's like saying Hitler had a bad day.
RENEE	People get caught up in things!

MAGGIE   Then they should get un-caught. You get in a
                bad situation, you walk away. You just...walk
                fucking...ay-way.

RENEE   Please stop using that word. It's bad in front of
                the children.

MAGGIE   The children are not present, Renee.

RENEE   Well, you don't watch your mouth even when
                they're here. —I can't walk away! How can I
                walk away!

MAGGIE   —I wasn't talking about John.

RENEE   Weren't you? He said you had a fight, he said
                you hate him. He says misery loves company,
                you'll try to get me to leave him, well, you can
                cut the crap, Maggie, just because you're lonely
                and frustrated...

MAGGIE   I've never interfered between you and John...

RENEE   Oh haven't you! Oh! haven't you...last week,
                when I was showing you that new dress, you got
                that look on your face, I could just tell what you
                were thinking—

MAGGIE   Because you were doing this cringing whelp
                act...you were cringing away—

RENEE   What...what act?

MAGGIE   Like a cringing whelp...a dog—

RENEE   That's another thing—

MAGGIE   "Oh John, I got this really cheap, see? See how
                cheap it was and I really do need it, oh you gruffy
                bear." Jesus—

RENEE	I do not sound like that!
MAGGIE	And you'd changed the sales tags—so he wouldn't know what you paid for the fucking dress!
RENEE	I do not sound like that!
MAGGIE	You sound like that!
RENEE	(*panting*) You don't understand.
MAGGIE	I understand.
RENEE	No. You don't. You don't understand.
MAGGIE	What is he, good in bed?
RENEE	Jealous?
MAGGIE	(*small laugh, gets up*) Maybe. That's it. Maybe. If a man came into me now he'll corrode in bile. He'd dissolve. I'll full of spleen. —Sorry. Sorry. Sorry. It's none of my business. It's none of my business. People don't know about married couples. I don't know about you and John. What really goes on. I can't talk.
RENEE	(*still furious*) No. You can't.
MAGGIE	No, I can't. I don't know, maybe you're right, it's this thing affecting everything. It's true, I can't stand the way he treats you. That's true.
RENEE	You don't understand. I like it.
MAGGIE	Do you?
RENEE	Yes.
MAGGIE	—Okay. Look, I'll water the plants, don't worry.

I'll take care of things.

RENEE   All right.

MAGGIE   (*pauses, then goes and embraces her*) Have a
            good time, have a great holiday.

RENEE   (*stiffly, unyielding*) Thanks.

            Go to black.

            Scene Five

            The darkened kitchen.

            *The hall light shines through into the
            kitchen.* MAGGIE *is at the sliding doors,
            key in lock. Opens doors, slides them back.
            She is in a housecoat. Switches on the light
            over the sink. Gets watering can and spray
            bottle from beside the sink. She measures
            hyponex into the watering can. Starts to
            water and spray plants. She moves about
            the house, then returns to the kitchen.
            Suddenly she bends over, grabs herself.*

MAGGIE   It's like living with a stone at your centre.
            Emma? Emma? I wish they'd find you dead.
            Yes I do. I wish it would just be over. I wish I
            could bury you and it would just be finished. I
            want my life to start again. I'm sorry. I can't
            mourn you, I can't grieve. I've just become mean
            minded. Small and petty and mean minded. I
            resent everyone their life. I resent Renee on a
            holiday in California, soaking up the sun,
            swimming. I resent her happiness. I resent her
            children. I grudge her that she has John to make
            love to at night. I grudge her that I can't love

anyone until I know where you are. I grudge
everything. I'm sorry. Be dead. Be something.
I can't stand it any more. (*turns and waters the
plants*)

> MAGGIE *goes out and into the hall,*
> *presumably upstairs.* RENEE *comes in*
> *from the hall, carrying bags. Stares wildly*
> *around, as if expecting some terrible*
> *devastation. She looks wild, crazed.* JOHN
> *comes after her, carrying a polystyrene*
> *freezer container, and a food hamper.*

JOHN   Why'd you run like that, you crazy or something?
              You coulda fallen and hurt yourself.

RENEE   She's watered the plants.

JOHN   She tells me to come home the middle a our
              friggin' vacation and that's why? She's afraid her
              friggin' lesbian friend's gonna forget ta water her
              friggin' plants?

RENEE   I was sick. I had to come home.

JOHN   She was sick. You are sick. You're crazy. I
              should have you put away in the funny farm.
              (*turns to go out, crosses to sliding doors*)

RENEE   Where're you going?

JOHN   To the car. To get the rest a our stuff. You left a
              lot a junk in the car.

RENEE   Don't wake Joanie, I'll get Joanie. I'll carry
              Joanie in.

JOHN   She's awake, she come in after me...she's
              upstairs.

RENEE   (*goes to hall, calls*) Joanie?! Joanie?! You in?!
               You upstairs?!

               No answer.

               (*calls*) Dougie?! Are you in, did you come in?

JOHN   They're dead on their feet, driving all day 'n' all
               night like maniacs.

               RENEE *stands there as if she can't remember
               what they have come home for. She reaches
               out to a plant, touches its leaf. It is still
               alive.*

RENEE   She took care of my plants.

JOHN   Ladybird ladybird
               Fly away home,
               Your house is on fire
               An' your children alone. (*laughs*)

               RENEE *covers her ears.*

               You disgust me. You're old. You're getting old.
               You fill me with disgust. I can't touch you, you
               make me want to throw up. (*turns and walks
               toward the sliding doors*)

               MAGGIE *comes in from the hall.* RENEE
               gives a small scream. JOHN *turns, stops.*

RENEE   What are you doing here? What are you doing
               here!

MAGGIE   I was upstairs. I was watering your plants.
               What's happened? Has something happened?

RENEE   What did you say to them, what did you say?

MAGGIE   What? What?

RENEE   What did you say to my children?

MAGGIE   —What? John?

> JOHN *comes back, shoves* RENEE *into a
> chair, gets her a drink, shoves it under her
> nose, forces her head back.*

RENEE   (*drinks, chokes*) No. I don't want it.

JOHN   You're hysterical. Can you hear me? You're
                hysterical. We're halfway down the coast of
                California and she says we gotta come home.
                Ladybird, ladybird, fly away home...

RENEE   Stop it.

MAGGIE   Renee, what happened?

JOHN   Nothing happened.

RENEE   Nothing happened. We just drove and drove,
                farther and farther away. Away. We just kept on
                driving... (*laughs*) Now we're home.

MAGGIE   Was there an accident?

RENEE   My life is an accident. (*laughs again*)

JOHN   Drink that. Drink that all down.

RENEE   (*to* MAGGIE) Oh hate me, for god's sake, hate
                me.

MAGGIE   Oh Renee, I don't hate you.

> MAGGIE *crosses to her and tries to hug her,
> but* RENEE *cannot bear her touch.*

I love you. You're my friend. I would have gone
mad these months without you. You're my
friend, my dear friend.

RENEE   No. No...(*sobs*)

MAGGIE   Why, why did you come home, what happened?

RENEE   Nothing. (*with terror*) Nothing happened. We
just drove further and further away. I watched the
signs going past...Sacramento...San Francisco
...Carmel...I watched the signs going past...(*a
long shuddering sigh*) I had to come home.

JOHN   She didn't like the signs. So she ruins a
vacation. I guess it's the Change, I guess she's
into the Change, you into the Change yet,
Maggie?

RENEE   Why don't you check things out, John. Why
don't you check things out. Maybe somebody's
broken in. Maybe something's happened.

JOHN   (*small laugh*) Nothing's happened.

RENEE   You haven't checked your workshop, John,
maybe something's gone, maybe something
belongs to you is gone.

JOHN   Nothing's gone.

RENEE   Maybe it's gone.

JOHN   —So, Maggie, sit down, have a drink, we haven't
seen you in a long time, any word?

MAGGIE   What?

JOHN   Any word on Emma?

MAGGIE   You'd have heard first thing, John.

JOHN   Sure we would, sure we would, I know that.
                (*small laugh*)

           MAGGIE *sits down beside* RENEE. *Looks
                at* JOHN.

                (*goes to cupboard, pours a drink for* MAGGIE)
                You get it out of her, Maggie, you're her best
                friend, you get it out of her, why she decides to
                ruin a perfectly good vacation. Here. (*hands*
                MAGGIE *the drink*)

           MAGGIE *takes it cautiously.*

                What you two got going anyway, she can't leave
                you for a couple of weeks, what you two got
                going anyway, eh? (*laughs*) Oh don't give me
                that look, Renee, I heard about these intellectuals,
                they swing both ways, eh, Maggie, eh? You
                swing both ways, don't you?

           MAGGIE *looks at* RENEE *who hasn't
                touched her drink.*

MAGGIE   Listen, are you okay? —If you want I can stay
                for a bit.

JOHN   Ooooh ho ho ho, oooo, I get it, I get it, I can
                take a hint, oooh ho, yes, I can take a hint, don't
                mind me, I'm leaving, I'm leaving. (*goes to
                sliding doors*)

           RENEE *stares after him. Rigid.*

                I know when I'm not wanted, I know when I am
                not wanted, yes sir. I'll leave you two girls
                together for girl talk, yes sir, I will leave you two
                girls together for a little old heart to heart.

MAGGIE   Renee? What is it?

JOHN   What is it, Renee, tell your best friend in the
world, eh? Why don't you, eh Renee? She's
your best friend in the world. Maggie, you
should watch out, people who come between
husband and wife get their face punched out
sometimes. (*holds up hand*) Unh, oh, no no,
just kidding, eh? Just kidding. You know the
kids missed Disneyland? The kids missed
Disneyland. We got all the way to Santa Barbara
almost and she says we gotta turn back. "We
gotta turn back, we gotta go home." (*laughs*)

MAGGIE   Well, I'm glad you're back, I missed you.

JOHN   Missed me, Maggie?

MAGGIE   Missed you both. Having you here. You know,
I came over every day to water your plants. It
was scary. I felt I had to come. I don't know
why. I just felt I had to come and check things.
It was a bit freaky.

JOHN   So.

> *He walks over to the cupboard and opens it.*
> *Takes out a couple of chocolate bars.*
> *Reaches into drinks cupboard, takes bottle of*
> *vodka.* RENEE *watches him.* JOHN *takes*
> *down a package of chips.* RENEE *watches*
> *him.*

Well, I got some stuff to do out in the workshop.
(*goes to sliding doors, looks at* RENEE, *walks*
out, slides door to)

MAGGIE   Listen, if you feel bad about what happened,
before you left, don't—I've been a drain on you, I
know. I've thought about it a lot while you've

been gone. I'm too dependent on you, I know
that, I'm going to be different. Listen, whatever
the reason, I'm glad you're back. I missed you.

RENEE *turns and looks at her.*

What, what is it? Renee?

RENEE   You're a fool. You're a fool you stupid cunt.
               You disgust me.

MAGGIE   You're tired, you're exhausted, let me help you—

RENEE   Get out. You stupid whore. You cunt. Get out.
               (starts to laugh and then sob)

MAGGIE *puts her arm around* RENEE *and
tries to help her from the room.* RENEE
pushes her away and goes into hall.

Go to black.

Scene Six

*Mid-October. On the fridge, children's
drawings of witches and jack-o'-lanterns are
held up with magnetic buttons.*

RENEE *comes in. It is early dusk. She
comes to the sliding doors and looks out.
Now she turns and goes to the fridge, starts
to get vegetables out of the bin. She gets a
piece of meat and she begins to pound it
with a wooden mallet. She seasons it, puts
it into a casserole. Puts in onions. Looks
up, holds herself, comes again to the sliding
doors and looks out. Picks up the telephone
and presses the intercom button. Waits.*

Looks again to the sliding doors. Waits.
Presses down the receiver button.

RENEE Hi. It's me. Just about to put the meat into the
microwave, thought I'd...(*listens*) John—
(*listens*) John, the last week or so you've bitched
about everything being overdone or cooked too
much, I'm just about ready to put this stuff into
the microwave, I thought I'd give you plenty of...
It's time to quit work! No, I did not. No, you
did not. No. No, I never heard you tell me not
to phone the shop. No. No. I told you, no.
(*turns and stares out sliding doors*) No, this isn't
some new idea she's put into my head. I said, I
haven't seen Maggie in weeks. John, I know
you're busy out there, what I want to know is,
what are you doing? You haven't shipped out a
chesterfield in a month! —Okay, okay. I am
minding my own business, I have to feed a
family, don't I? Jenkins phoned again yesterday
and said where was his armchair, that came in last
August. You haven't even paid the hydro! I told
you, Maggie hasn't even been here in...five
weeks now. This is me, me, Renee talking. All
I'm saying is, the dinner's going into the
microwave, so could you be in here on time
tonight?

She lifts her finger off receiver button.
Presses intercom button. Waits. Looks
toward sliding doors. Waits.

John? It's just me, I thought I'd tell you, dinner's
going into the microwave now. —I didn't think
you'd mind just this once. Well, you haven't
eaten your dinner the last few...all right, John.
All right, all right, all right I won't, no I won't.
I'm sorry. I'm...sorry.

Slowly she puts the receiver back onto the

> *wall hook. Lifts receiver again. Dials three numbers. Puts receiver back onto hook. Puts casserole of meat into microwave.* MAGGIE *knocks at sliding doors. Slides them back.*

MAGGIE   Hi.

RENEE   Oh. Hi.

MAGGIE   (*halfway in*) How are you?

RENEE   I'm all right. You?

MAGGIE   So so. —Well, just thought I'd see how you were, saw your light on...

RENEE   Want a drink?

MAGGIE   Well...

RENEE   He's out in the shop.

MAGGIE   Well, maybe a quick one.

RENEE   Guess you've been pretty busy—

MAGGIE   I've been pretty busy...

> *They laugh.* RENEE *makes her a drink.*

I've missed you.

RENEE   Yeah. Well. It's just one of those things. (*hands her the drink*) We really don't have that much in common. I took a couple a courses but John's right, I'm not in your league.

MAGGIE   John's not always right, Renee.

RENEE

Yeah, well, that's another thing; you always saying stuff like that, it could break us up, you know? John and I. John and me, which is it anyway?

MAGGIE

(*looks at her drink, puts it down*) Yeah. Well. Guess I better be going. (*starts for sliding doors*)

RENEE

How...are things?

MAGGIE

Shitty. Oh, I get up, I move, I go to work, I lecture, I even make jokes. Time goes by. I don't hear her screaming anymore.

RENEE

What?

MAGGIE

Sometimes at night I thought I heard her scream.

RENEE

—Stay and have your drink.

MAGGIE

Was that what it was, my buttinsky stuff about John?

RENEE

Oh, you meant well...

MAGGIE

No I didn't. Maybe I didn't. Maybe what happened has made me so paranoid about men. I don't know.

RENEE

Only it came to a choice kind of, between you and him, he.

MAGGIE

(*breaks into a laugh*) Him. It's him, you had it right the first time, why don't you just relax, you'll be okay, you have a feel for language, you know.

RENEE

Do I?

MAGGIE

Yes. —You always pretend to be so stupid,

Renee, it kind of pisses me off, if you want to know.

RENEE   Oh yes?

MAGGIE   Yes. I mean, if it's time for truth games, I might as well tell you, this habit you've got of putting yourself down all the time, and this invidious comparison stuff you're into about me, it really pisses me off.

RENEE   Invidious comparison. I don't know what that means.

MAGGIE   You know what it means. Look. If you wanted an education, a formal education, you could get one, what's stopping you? Don't put it off onto...no, I know what you're going to say...but this house practically runs itself and you could go in, even for day courses. John's always around anyway, you don't have to worry about Joanie and Dougie, there'd always be someone home for them.

RENEE   (*a shrill laugh*) You don't know what you're talking about.

MAGGIE   —If you're that unhappy, leave him. Oh there I go again. Boy. Put my foot into it everytime, it's just, I can't stand seeing you take it from him, I just can't stand it, it's horrible, it's so degrading. —I mean, have you got the TV fixed yet? No, no? There you are, you see? You were begging him to let you get it fixed how long ago, and just because he's out in the shop day and night doesn't mean you have to go without TV for you and the kids, I mean why doesn't he let you watch his set in the shop? I mean, it's crazy the way you have to beg for everything!

RENEE   What?

MAGGIE   The way you have to beg for everything, the way
         you have to cringe and grovel, and *apologize* for
         every blessed thing, you think I didn't hear you
         apologizing for spending so much on Joanie's
         school shoes.

RENEE   What TV?

MAGGIE   Your TV, haven't you got it fixed yet?

RENEE   No, you said he's got a TV in the shop, what
         TV?

MAGGIE   The one he took in last summer. He's got it
         hooked up to your cable line. I know because he
         bragged to me, he didn't have to pay twice, he
         knew how to hook it up, said he could hook it up
         to Pay-TV with some aluminum foil.

RENEE   John's got a TV in the shop?

MAGGIE   Oh, I don't know. I'm out of line I guess. I'm
         sorry. I said to myself, Keep your mouth shut,
         don't say a word, and here we are, right into it
         again.

RENEE   I didn't know about the TV.

MAGGIE   Well, he's gotta be doing something in there, he's
         in there day and night, isn't he? I guess he
         watches the TV in there.

RENEE   We have a good marriage. You have no right to
         say anything about our marriage.

MAGGIE   You have a rotten marriage.

RENEE   Get out of here. I didn't ask you in. I curse the day you moved next door. I curse you.

MAGGIE   What is it, Renee, tell me what it is.

RENEE   We were happy until you came. We were happy.

MAGGIE   He treats you like shit.

RENEE   He's right about you, you're green with envy.

MAGGIE   The day I envy you a man like that prick—

RENEE   You're dying for it.

MAGGIE *laughs.*

Don't you dare laugh at me, you big shot...you think you're perfect—

MAGGIE   Oh go to hell, go to hell. I've missed you, I've missed you terribly.

RENEE   Last week, Dougie was late home from school. The bus came and he wasn't on it. I was watching from the window, and I saw the bus come and drop off the Fraser kids, but Dougie wasn't on the bus. Joanie was going to be late because she had band practice, so I knew she'd be late, but Dougie was supposed to be on the bus. I phoned the school and Mrs. Duncan had kept him late. He'd thrown rocks during recess and she'd kept him late. —She said she didn't know he was supposed to come home on the bus. She said it was inexcusable of her. She apologized. —Dougie walked all the way home from school. He got here, he was half crying, he had ran all the way the last part, he knew I'd be worried sick about him. He had ran all the last part, he could hardly breathe.

MAGGIE   The terror.

RENEE   Yes. And that was just a few minutes. Less than
                15 minutes before I got Mrs. Duncan on the
                phone. That was...and all these months, you...

                        MAGGIE *nods, holding herself in.*

                It's true, I've always been jealous of you, it's true,
                you seemed to have it so good, you were so
                lucky, you were so free.

                        MAGGIE *stiffens although* RENEE *does not
                        notice.*

MAGGIE   Fortune's child.

RENEE   (*unaware of the change*) Part of me was glad
                when you were brought down.

MAGGIE   —That's the basis of most dramatic literature.
                They love it when Oedipus falls down, you
                know, they get a secret nasty thrill when they
                know he's slept with his mother. (*small laugh*)

                        RENEE *steps away, realizes she's gone too
                        far. The two women look at each other.
                        The hostility re-flares.*

RENEE   Well, I wouldn't know, I don't have your advanced
                knowledge of dramatic literature.

MAGGIE   (*closes her eyes*) Oh shit. Here we go again.
                I've lost my child, Renee. I've lost my child.
                My child could be anywhere, terrible things could
                be happening to her right now, while we fight
                out this old old story about who's got the better
                education...I don't believe you sometimes.

RENEE   I don't believe *you* walk in here, you haven't even stopped by in five weeks—

MAGGIE Jesus, the last time I was here you called me a
cunt.

RENEE You bust in here, you try to get between me and
John, what've you got against John anyway?

MAGGIE Let's not get started.

RENEE You've got something against him, you've looked
down on him from the first, you have, I can
remember that first night, after we'd been talking
for a couple of weeks, and I invited you over—

MAGGIE Emma and me.

RENEE (*small smile*) Isn't it *Emma and I?*

MAGGIE (*stares at her*) No, actually, that was the
objective case.

RENEE Oh was it?

MAGGIE Yes, it was. Personally, I don't very much give a
good fuck about the objective case, but it comes
naturally to me, while the ablative absolute does
not.

RENEE Oooh ho.

MAGGIE You want to know what I've got against John,
you really want to know? That night, that night
when we had dinner together, he put you down for
every single thing you did, he put you down and
he smiled this small little complicit smile at me
as if I'd understand why he was doing it. This
small little you-and-me-babe smile at me.

RENEE What kind of smile?

MAGGIE   You-and-me-Babe, we-know-the-kind-of-dumb-bitch-we've-got-here smile.

RENEE   No, that other word. I don't understand what you say! You do it on purpose!

MAGGIE   What word?

RENEE   You know what word! How am I supposed to go out into the world? I can't make it without a man! I can't, I don't have your chances.

MAGGIE   Shit shit shit, Renee, that's shit and you know it's shit, and I won't have this envy, this rotten fucking envy, I won't let it eat away at you and me, I won't, I won't! (*goes to her, but angrily, and puts her arms around* RENEE)

RENEE   You're trying to bust us up. (*tries to resist* MAGGIE*'s embrace*) It's true what he says, you're just trying to get in between us, you're making me think things about him, it's you...(*starts to sob*) Oh god, oh god.

        MAGGIE *is holding on grimly.*

        Oh god, oh god, oh I can't bear it. I can't stand it, Maggie, I can't live...(*buries her face in* MAGGIE*'s breast*)

            JOHN *appears at sliding doors, watches. Opens the doors.* MAGGIE *starts, begins to draw back guiltily, then reaffirms her embrace of* RENEE, *and stares defiantly at* JOHN. RENEE, *at first, is unaware.* JOHN *comes in and stands silently, watching. Grins.* RENEE, *after a moment, senses his presence, and moves away.* MAGGIE *looks at her in fury.*

It's almost ready. Dinner. —I'll get you a beer.

> *She goes to fridge and gets JOHN a beer,*
> *opens it. Gets a glass. MAGGIE stands*
> *still, looks at JOHN. He grins at MAGGIE.*
> *RENEE holds out glass of beer to JOHN,*
> *who doesn't take it. RENEE puts it down*
> *on table beside the place setting.*

MAGGIE   I'd better go then.

> *She comes toward sliding doors, but JOHN*
> *is in her way. She pauses.*

Excuse me.

> *JOHN raises his hand abruptly. MAGGIE*
> *winces and cowers.*

JOHN   (*laughs*) What's the matter, Maggie, I was just
going to take off my cap. Dja think I was going
to hitya? She thought I was going to give her a
knuckle sandwich, Renee. Didja see her? Jeezus,
Maggie thought I was goingta give her an old
knuckle sandwich, the old one-two, what's the
matter, Maggie, got a guilty conscience? I was
just taking off my cap, see?

MAGGIE   Just let me get by, please.

JOHN   I ain't stoppin' ya, Maggie, who's stoppin' ya?
You can get by.

RENEE   Let her get by, John.

JOHN   Another country heard from—another cuntree
heard from, get it, Maggie? You're the big
professor, you should like wordplay, another cunt
tree, get it?

MAGGIE   Why do you always do that, John? Talk like a
                moron when I'm here.

JOHN   (*laughs*) Do I, talk like a moron, Maggie?

MAGGIE   Yes. You speak perfectly good English and then
                I come over and suddenly it's Dogpatch Time.

JOHN   Dogpatch Time, eh? That's pretty good, ain't it,
                Renee? Dogpatch Time.

RENEE   Let her go, John. Just let her go.

                    JOHN *moves suddenly aside, with a sweep
                    of his cap.*

MAGGIE   I know you, John, I know you from when I was a
                kid in Winnipeg, there was this boy there,
                Norman Stewart, he used to grab the little ones
                and give them an Indian Wrist Burn. (*exits*)

                    JOHN *turns and watches her go.* RENEE,
                    behind him, closes her eyes. JOHN *very
                    casually closes the sliding doors. Crosses to
                    table and sits down.*

JOHN   Well? You said supper was going to be ready.

RENEE   (*with an effort, goes to microwave and gets out
                the food*) Oh. I'm sorry, I forgot the vegetables.

                    *She puts in the vegetable dish. Punches the
                    computer. Puts the casserole on the table.*

JOHN   No beer? (*politely*)

                    RENEE *goes to table and gets the beer and
                    lifts it toward him.*

                Thank you. (*refuses to take it*)

> RENEE *is forced to put it down beside him on the table beside his hand.*

Well. So you and your friend have made up, eh?
That's good. I like for you to have friends.
Bosom buddies again eh? (*small laugh, lifts casserole dish*) My my, what's this?

RENEE   Lasagna.

JOHN   Lasagna. My my. Lasagna. What'd the kids have?

RENEE   They ate before.

JOHN   I didn't ask when they ate, Renee, I asked what did they eat? There's a grammatical distinction. There's a semantic distinction, which I am sure your dear friend Maggie could elucidate upon. What did they eat, the children?

RENEE   Peanut butter sandwiches.

JOHN   Peanut butter sandwiches. And I get lasagna. Excuse me, Renee, but this is not really anything so fancy as lasagna, this is hamburger and macaroni. No. Come here and look at it, Renee, this is hamburger and macaroni.

RENEE   (*as bell dings*) The vegetables are ready.

JOHN   It never fails to amaze me how you cannot understand what I am saying to you. Did I inquire about the state of the vegetables? Did I? Did I.

RENEE   No.

JOHN   No, I asked you to kindly step over here and look at this dish, which you claim is lasagna. Step over here, Maggie.

> RENEE *crosses to table.*

Bend over and look at it, Maggie.

RENEE   Please.

JOHN   Look at it, Maggie.

RENEE   My name is Renee.

> JOHN *grabs her by the neck and pushes her*
> *face into the casserole.*

JOHN   That is shit. This is shit, that's what it is, you
           give me shit to eat, you filthy bitch.

RENEE   You don't give me any money! (*backs away,*
           teeth chattering, but ferocious) You never give
           me any money, that's all I got in the freezer,
           that's why the kids don't even get hamburger, and
           you got a TV in the workshop!

JOHN   What?

RENEE   You heard me, you got a TV in the shop. (*grabs*
           a tea towel and tries to wipe her face)

JOHN   I got a what?

RENEE   (*standing against the sink*) If you touch me, I'll
           do something.

JOHN   I don't think I heard you right, Renee. I got a
           what in the shop?

RENEE   A TV.

JOHN   Oh? How you know that, Renee?

RENEE   I had to go in today. To get a washer.

JOHN   Oh yes? A washer? A washer for what?

RENEE   For the sink. For the bathroom sink. The tap
                 in there.

JOHN   A washer. For the bathroom sink.

RENEE   I don't need to bother you for a washer put in, I
                 can put one in myself. I don't need to worry you
                 for that.

JOHN   Which tap is that, Renee?

RENEE   The one in the bathroom. It's leaking.

JOHN   I gathered it was the one in the bathroom. You
                 told me that before.

RENEE   The one in the shower. The right one.

JOHN   The right one?

RENEE   I mean, hot, the hot one.

                 JOHN *pushes back his chair.* RENEE
                 jumps.

JOHN   (*crosses to her, smiles*) Don't give me any of
                 your lies, Renee. You weren't in the shop.

RENEE   Yes, I was. I was.

JOHN   No, Renee, you were not.

RENEE   I saw it.

JOHN   (*backhands her casually*) No, Renee.

RENEE   (*falls to her knees*) Oh don't oh don't oh
               don't...the kids'll hear again...oh god...

                    JOHN *kicks her in the stomach.*

               Oh don't John...I'm sorry...oh god...

JOHN   (*pulls her up by the hair*) Okay Renee? Okay?
               Now you tell me the truth, Renee. I have to do
               this when you lie to me. You know that. I have
               to hurt you when you lie to me, Renee, now you
               tell me.

                    He knees her in the chest. Catches her as
                    she falls back, keeps her upright.

RENEE   Maggie.

JOHN   Ah. Maggie told you. Yeah. She saw me take
               it in.

RENEE   It isn't fair.

JOHN   What? Did I hear you make a comment?

RENEE   The kids don't have TV.

JOHN   You're an old whore, Renee, and I can do what I
               like with you and you'll take it, because you're an
               old whore and I'm the last chance you've got for a
               real man. That's true, isn't it? Renee?

RENEE   I'm not an...oooh.

JOHN   Yes, you are. Say it. (*pulls her hair back*)

RENEE   —I'm...an old—

JOHN   Whore.

RENEE   Whore...and you're the last...chance I got—

JOHN   For a real man.

RENEE   ...a real man...

JOHN   Now, Renee, I'm going to have to punish you, you know that, don't you? You know I've got to punish you now, don't you? Yes. Okay. Take it out. Go on. Take it out.

> RENEE *sobs.* JOHN *pulls her hair backwards until her face is close to his crotch.*

Go on, Renee, don't make it hard on yourself. (*laughs*) Make it hard on me.

> RENEE *reaches up and unzips him.*

That's a good girl. That's a good girl.

> *Go to black.*

Scene Seven

Halloween night. The workshop.

A very small area of the workshop is visible. We can see a bit of the work bench. The tools hanging on a perforated board. Nothing is out of place. There is a plastic filing cabinet arrangement for nuts, bolts, etc.

Immediately to one side of the work bench and lathe is a piece of the floor, painted a bright blue. On top of this floor area are

*plastic jugs filled with various fluids: oil
for wood, paint thinner, etc.*

*Slowly, the lights are brought up on
RENEE looking at the area, from the
penumbra.*

*RENEE looks at the workshop. —She
cannot see a TV.*

*She is wearing a housedress, and has made
herself up carefully: neat and clean and
ordinary-looking.*

*She comes into the light. Stands in front of
the lathe. She touches the lathe, the tools,
the filing cabinet of small items. Turns
away, then turns back. She looks at the
plastic jugs on the square of blue painted
floor. The floor is painted a slightly
brighter blue than the surrounding area. She
turns away again. Can't think why she is
bothered. Starts away. Stops. Turns back.
Something else was there before. What was
it? She looks around. Yes, something else
had stood there. She goes over to the jugs.
She bends to lift one. It does not come
away. It is glued to the piece of flooring
which she sees now is a wooden plywood
slab, fitted into the floor.*

*Behind her a silhouette...the figure of a man,
as if in a doorway.*

RENEE straightens up. Does not turn.

JOHN   (*comes in*) Looking for something?

RENEE   You know that tarnish-free stuff? I was looking
                for that tarnish-free stuff.

JOHN	Why would I have tarnish-free stuff?
RENEE	I needed it for my rings. (*holds out her hands*)
JOHN	Gold doesn't tarnish.
RENEE	Not my wedding ring, this ring, the one Dougie gave me.
JOHN	The one Dougie gave you.
RENEE	It's turning my finger green! (*laughs, shows him*)
JOHN	(*refuses to look at her hand*) I don't like you messing around in the workshop.
RENEE	Where's the TV?
JOHN	What?
RENEE	Where's the TV, John?
JOHN	I took it back. I was watching it too much, I wasn't getting my work done. —Listen, don't worry, I'll get the kids' TV fixed. I'll take it into the shop today. Is that what's bugging you?
RENEE	Is that Jenkins' armchair?
JOHN	Oh yeah. I had to wait for this part.
RENEE	You had a nightmare again last night.
JOHN	—We got a good life, Renee, you and me, we got a good life for us 'n' the kids. We got our ups and downs but we're a lucky family, you know that? We got our health. I got this little business, it'll start picking up again, I know I'm good at what I do, I'm good with my hands, the

thing is, you see, I'm really like everybody else.
That's what you don't understand about me,
Renee. I'm just like anybody else. I know you
judge me, yes, you judge me, you have always
judged me! —but I am just like any man. Just
like any man. I have my pride, Renee, you can't
undermine a man's pride in his manhood, that's
what you have done.

RENEE   How did I do that?

JOHN   A lot of couples, they can't talk things over like
             we can, they have a communication problem, we
             don't have a communication problem, we talk,
             you and I. —A man sometimes has problems
             that way, that's all. It's quite natural. You ask
             any psychologist.

RENEE   I am not complaining about that, have I ever said
             anything about that?

JOHN   You're not an educated woman, Renee, you don't
             understand these things, a man goes through
             many stages in his life. Many stages in his life.
             There's a book called that: *Stages in Life's Way*
             or something. By Kierkegaard. Have you read
             Stage in Life's Way, by Kierkegaard? Did you
             realize that if God exists, Renee, it is our duty to
             deny him? —Have you read Heidegger? Have
             you read Jaspers? I'm an educated man. I've had
             to educate myself. You know Dostoyevsky once
             said that only if you could rape a 10-year-old girl
             could you say you were truly free. Free of all
             morality. It's conventional morality that holds us
             back, Renee. I married you although I knew you
             were a conventional woman.

RENEE   Why would anyone want to?

JOHN   I married you knowing full well there would be

areas of my life you could not enter, areas in my life you could not understand, but you married me, you took an oath, for richer or poorer, for better or worse, we are one flesh, Renee. Why would anyone want to what?

RENEE   Rape a 10-year-old girl?

JOHN   You don't understand the concept, Renee. Listen, listen, you know what Maggie said that time about Emma—

RENEE   Emma?

JOHN   You know what she said, how Emma believed what Anne Frank believed, how she used to say those lines..."because in spite of everything, I still believe that people are really good at heart"? You know. Maggie quoted that to us, she said Emma believed that. But listen! Maggie said those lines were the last lines in the book. —They're not. No. And I've heard that from other people too, people say that all the time, that those're the last lines in the book, but they're not. You know what Anne Frank talks about at the end of the book? No, those lines come earlier, a couple of chapters, I think, no, what she's talking about at the end of the book is how she can't be good, how she knows she can't ever really be a good person. People don't like to know that Anne Frank knew it, and what she says at the end of the book is she could be good, yes, she could be, "if only there weren't any people living in the world." Something like that, I haven't maybe got it exact: I could be good if..."there weren't any other people living in the world." That's what it says at the very end of that book. —You see? Do you see, Renee?

RENEE   She wasn't a good person? Anne Frank wasn't a

	good person? So it was okay what they did to her?
JOHN	—It makes me tired sometimes, Renee, to try to make you understand a philosophical concept.
RENEE	You're trying to say Anne Frank wasn't a good person?
JOHN	That's right. Nobody is, Renee, that's what I am trying to convey to you.
RENEE	So she can be raped?
JOHN	What? What are you talking about, Anne Frank wasn't raped.
RENEE	You said this guy said you should rape a 10-year-old girl.
JOHN	On, no, that was just an example of the act that would be a defiance...would spit in the face of God, which is the duty of a free person. You see, Abraham should have given God the finger. You know. You have heard of Abraham, Renee.
RENEE	Yes.
JOHN	When he took up poor little Isaac to the mountaintop, and God said Kill your only son, and you can imagine how difficult that was, Sarah was 99 when she had him, how old was Abraham? I don't know, who cares, don't get me off the track, the point of all this is, Abraham should have refused to obey God.
RENEE	But there was a ram in the thicket.
JOHN	What—? Yes, but how did Abraham know that?

RENEE	He had faith.
JOHN	(*laughs*) A lot of good that did Anne Frank. Listen, if you want to know the truth about Emma, that was her trouble, she believed in people, she trusted people, Maggie taught her to trust people, that was her trouble. In a way, the person who teaches her that lesson is a saviour, an educator, yes, an educator, she could be grateful the rest of her life. Even Moses said you should rape the young girls. In Numbers. You didn't know that, did you? Oh yes, when they were going against some tribe, he said kill off all the older women, the ones who are dirty already. That means the ones who have done it with men. But then take the pure girls for yourself. Moses understood that that's what women really want. That's what you want, isn't it, Renee?
RENEE	I thought I did.
JOHN	Oh you did. You loved the rough and tumble, admit it.
RENEE	Yes. I admit it.
JOHN	Then you think you're a married woman, you get all respectable and you pretend you don't want it. But I remember.
RENEE	Only, it wasn't like it is now.
JOHN	Sure it is. —You and I, we get along, Renee. You can't follow me everywhere, that's only natural, you don't have the education, and to tell you the truth, you're just not as bright as I am, but that's okay, I'll look after you. —Only. Renee? Don't come into the workshop anymore, okay? Okay, Baby? I like to keep things a certain way. Anything you want you ask me for

it, I'll get it. In fact, hey wait a minute—where is that tarnish-free? I did have it, I had it for something on that armoire I was doing—just a moment. Aha! (*gets the tarnish-free bottle and hands it to her*) You were right, kiddo, this time you were absolutely right, it was here all along!

RENEE   I can't believe anybody said that, rape a 10-year-old girl, I want to read that book where he says that.

JOHN   Okay. I'll get it for you. It's down...in the basement.

RENEE   Where?

JOHN   Downstairs in the basement, in that box my mother sent over. I'll get it for you, but it's really a sort of metaphor you know. It doesn't mean literally.

RENEE   You took back the TV eh?

JOHN   Yes. Months ago.

RENEE   Okay. (*turns to go*)

JOHN   Don't worry, I'll take the one in the house in, I'll take it in this aft. The kids'll have it tonight.

RENEE   It's Halloween tonight. They'll be out tonight.

JOHN   Halloween eh? Jesus, time flies, doesn't it, it's quite warm still though, Indian summer eh?

RENEE   Yes. (*pauses*) That'd be nice though, John, if you could do that, for the kids. —I miss it too, the TV.

JOHN   Okay okay. A promise is a promise. Okay?

RENEE   Okay. (*goes out*)

                  JOHN looks after her. Turns and looks down at the jugs on the plywood slab. Now he looks out after RENEE.

                  Go to black.

Scene Eight

Halloween night. The kitchen.

RENEE is preparing bowls of candies, apples, pennies, for the children. From the front room the sound of the TV can be heard.

RENEE   (*briskly*) Dougie? Joanie? Now you can listen to that TV anytime. —You're going out tonight, do you hear me? I didn't put hours into those costumes for nothing. Now you get ready. I'm coming in and turning that TV off in 10 seconds. I'm not kidding. 10...9...8...7...6...5...4...3...2...1!—

                  The sound of the TV goes off. She turns back to get the bowls. As she goes out into the hall the ring of the doorbell is heard.

See? They've started already!

                  Door opens. Children's voices: "Trick or treat!"

(*off*) Well! Don't you look horrible! Oooh! You scare me sick. Oooh...what a face! Here, please take it and go away...

Laughter from children. Door shuts.

(*reappears in kitchen*) Oh I forgot the pennies for Unicef. Joanie? Joanie, are the kids still taking pennies for Unicef? Joanie, answer me when I talk to you. (*goes into hall for a moment, comes back*) I thought they were.

She looks at telephone. Picks it up. Then, puts it down firmly.

Okay. I'm coming. (*goes out, off*) Yes, that's good, yes, oh that bag's big enough, oh all right. (*comes back to kitchen, gets a big plastic bag, takes it out to hall*) Now I want you two sticking together, no, Dougie, I do not want you leaving your sister, No, listen to me! I don't care, you are not to leave your sister. Joanie? I am not listening to any of that, things're going to be different around here from now on, I'm not taking any lip from you, no! And back here by nine at the latest. Joanie, do you understand me? All right. All right. Yes, you look lovely. Yes. I love you. Take care. Don't get sick!

Door opens.

Listen, don't bother Mrs. Webb, she's sick. Yes. She's dying. So don't go up to her place, okay? Okay.

Door shuts. RENEE *comes back into the kitchen. Sits at the table. Gets up, goes to stove, puts on kettle. Doorbell rings. She goes out. Door opens.*

Hello! Don't you look wonderful! Here you are.

Children's voices: "Trick or treat!"

Door shuts. RENEE comes back. Sits at
table. She stares out through the sliding
doors. Kettle sings. She gets up and turns
it off. She doesn't make tea. She stares out
the sliding doors. Doorbell rings. She
almost doesn't respond. Then she does. We
hear door open: "Trick or treat!"

Oh my! My goodness, oh that's really ugly,
Bennie. Oh I'm sorry, it's not Bennie, I thought
maybe it was Bennie Fraser from down the street,
but you can't be Bennie, you're too disgusting.

Laughter. Door shuts. She comes back and
stares out the sliding doors. She laughs.
Goes to the telephone.

(*on telephone*) This is Mrs. John Gifford.
1600 Ashcroft Road. My husband is going to
commit suicide. He's in his workshop. He's
locked himself in with a gun. —1600 Ashcroft
Road. That's just off the highway. A sort of
lane. A *cul de sac*. Never mind. You just turn
off the highway about five miles from the park,
going east. —298-6009. 20 minutes ago. Yes
he did.

Hangs up the receiver. Goes and sits at the
table. Folds her hands and rests them on the
table. Stares out the sliding doors. MAGGIE
appears at the sliding doors. RENEE starts,
then sees who it is. MAGGIE knocks
tentatively, then opens the doors.

MAGGIE   Hi! I thought I'd come help. I brought some
stuff.

She has some Halloween goodies with her in
a bag. She goes to RENEE's cupboards and

takes down bowls to put her stuff in.

Listen. I've got an apology to make. Listen, Renee, I'm sorry, I think I set you up for something. I think when I left here the other night I got him mad and I knew he'd take it out on you. It's been bugging the hell out of me. I don't even know why I did it. I knew he'd take it out on you. He did, didn't he?

Doorbell rings.

Oh let me get it. I put out all the lights at my place. (*goes out into hall*)

Door opens: "Trick or treat!"

(*off*) Hi! Oh my! Oh what a gruesome pair! Oh Jeez, Renee, you should see these two! Oh where did you get *that*! Yuck.

Laughter. Door shuts. RENEE all the time sits staring at the sliding doors, her hands clasped.

(*comes back into the kitchen*) At first I thought I couldn't stand Halloween and then I thought, Oh Hell, I'll just go over to Renee's. Are the kids collecting for Unicef this year?

RENEE   Mmm-hmm.

MAGGIE   He did take it out on you, didn't he? And I knew it. Jesus, I'm such a shit.

RENEE   (*small laugh*) You did me a favour. Now he'll do anything for me. I've got something on him, now he can't do enough for me, he got the TV fixed.

MAGGIE	Oh. That's good. I guess. What did you have to pay for it?
RENEE	(*small laugh*) Plenty.

Doorbell rings.

Too much.

MAGGIE	(*going to the hall*) Let me get this one, eh?
RENEE	Too fucking much.

Children's voices: "Trick or treat!"

MAGGIE   (*off*) Ooooh...You look wonderful. Just beautiful. My goodness. Oh you're a real stunner. Does your mother know you're out?

      RENEE *makes an hysterical sound. The first break she's made.*

There you are. Bye now.

Door shuts.

(*comes back to kitchen*) God, they're so cute. *Walpurgisnacht.* All Saints' Eve. How we make the horrible ordinary. How we transform it, make it comic and cuddly. Human beings!

RENEE	Wal what?
MAGGIE	*Walpurgisnacht*...it means night of the witches. Something like that.
RENEE	Oh.
MAGGIE	Night of the female bitches. Oh the old chthonic underpinnings of this society...I love Halloween

really. I always did, as a child. We don't really
have enough times to let go...ritual times of
release...I guess Christmas is the time we really
let go...remember how drunk we got last
Christmas?...how disgusted Emma was with us?

RENEE   I remember John kissed you, under the mistletoe.

MAGGIE   Yes.

RENEE   You seemed to enjoy it.

MAGCIE   Well, you can be attracted to a man...

RENEE   Then you got into this thing about open
        mortgages.

MAGGIE   Oh yes, jesus.

        Doorbell rings.

You want to go?

        RENEE *shakes her head.* MAGGIE *goes*
        into hall. Opens door: "Trick or treat."

Aw...aw, Renee, you should see these
ones...there's a ghost and a skeleton and a
monster mummy...is that what you are, a
monster mummy? Oh my...here you go...Bye
now. Bye.

        Door shuts. MAGGIE *returns.*

(*shakes her head*) Normalization of our deepest
terrors. That's part of it.

RENEE   You started in about how you had this open
        mortgage and John didn't know what you were
        talking about. And he said he'd paid off more

than half of the house and you said how long had he owned it and he said 10 years and you said if he didn't have an open mortgage that would probably be impossible. And he got out the contract and you showed him, he hadn't been paying off the...what did you call it...the principal? He hadn't been paying off the principal at all, he'd just been paying off the interest, keeping just ahead of it really, and you said unless he got himself an open mortgage he couldn't pay off at his own rate, he was at the mercy of the mortgage company, and he was furious with you, did you know that? And he went down to check it out and you were right, and he couldn't even get an open mortgage, there weren't any and he said you must have done something fast, no, pulled a fast one to get an open mortgage, and then you came over and he said, Show me, and you did, you showed him. —God he hated you for that. And every month he would sign the damn cheque and he would figure it out, how much off the principal and it was only 18 dollars or something, it would drive him crazy. And then you bought that chesterfield. —I think that's when he started to go down.

MAGGIE   Go down...what is it, Renee?

RENEE   Oh yes, he started slacking off on his work, you know, and he spent so much time out in the shop. But nothing was really getting done. Oh everything was tidy. He organized everything. He spent hours, days, organizing screws and bolts and stuff. It was crazy. That was about February. The thing was, I always knew about the shop, it was in the house description when we got the place, so I always knew.

          Doorbell rings. RENEE gets up and goes

out to hall. Door opens. Children's voices: "Trick or treat!"

Here you are.

      MAGGIE gets herself a drink from cupboard. Gets ice cubes from fridge. Sound of door closing. RENEE reappears.

Get me one too, would you?

MAGGIE	Sure. (*makes her a drink*) You're in a mood tonight.
RENEE	Night of bitches. (*small laugh*)
MAGGIE	I don't get what you said just before, about the house description. You said something and I didn't quite—
RENEE	Tell me about Emma.
MAGGIE	What?
RENEE	No, you think you know someone, you live beside them for a few years, but you don't know them, tell me about Emma, who was she?
MAGGIE	Emma was a 12-year-old girl. She hated it when I got the divorce. The sun rose and set on Graham. It didn't matter what I said or how I felt, and the truth is, Graham isn't a bad man, I just didn't want him anymore. And, and, and, she was religious...she had this big religious streak... probably connected with puberty...she prayed for people...she believed everyone has good in them ...I don't know, I probably encouraged that...we had a talk once and I said if there's a choice...and you could choose between the one who fools and the one who's fooled, it's better to choose the one

who's fooled, because then you've put your bet on humanity, and that is like inertia...it starts something...people respond to trust...oh god, I may have made her a walking target for some creep.

RENEE   How would you describe me, if somebody asked, if I were dead or something and somebody asked?

MAGGIE   (*sips drink*) Well. I'd say, you were my friend. Your name was Renee, short for Maureen, Gifford. You'd been married once before, had two kids. Were raped once. Met John, married him, but I guess that's just data isn't it? Well, I'd say you had a good sense of humour, and a quick wit, but you were frustrated, you felt inadequate about your education, you felt inferior to other people, and it niggled at you because you knew if you had a chance you'd be okay. —No, I'd say you were a woman torn between things. Torn. Not knowing which way to go, and caught in the middle.

RENEE   Is that what you'll say?

MAGGIE   Well, it was a bit off the cuff, I'm sure I could work up something better if I had to do your eulogy. I'd say, Renee was a good friend to me.

RENEE   Is that what you'll say.

MAGGIE   You planning on going somewhere?

RENEE   In the end, we're all just part of someone else's scenario, aren't we? I'm real to you as the neighbour who stuck by you when your daughter went missing. That's what it comes to, I'm just a character in your scenario. Someone you tried to help out, because she wasn't liberated.

Someone who had a yen for education but was "torn."

MAGGIE   Well, you asked for it quick. I...you mean more to me than that.

RENEE   But even with Emma, in the end it's not Emma who's real to you, it's what you said wrong to her, what you did wrong, that's what's real...

MAGGIE   Oh Emma is real. —Oh yes. Emma is real. Although sometimes now I can't remember how her face looked. She had a mole right here (*indicates thigh*)...I used to notice it when I did her diapers...and then of course in the last years she's been so modest, she never let me see her naked...I never saw it... Sometimes I think her god wants me to curse him and die. But I won't, I won't, won't give her god that satisfaction, won't admit her god exists. Not even to curse him. A twist on Job. But you're right—she's becoming somebody in my *scenario*. Jesus I hate words like that.

RENEE   (*drinks*) I have all these vocabulary entries from my one venture into higher education.

MAGGIE   Oh, when your child is taken from you the world ought to end. The world ought to end. I ought to have died from the pain of it. (*takes out pack of cigarettes and lights one*)

                RENEE *reaches over to the cupboard and pulls out an ashtray for her.*

                That's what's so surprising, I went on living. It's not as though I had hope left. No, it's not as though I have hope left. Not now. I think, by the summer, I knew she had to be dead. She would have called me. One night, that was the night you came back, I came over here to water your plants, I thought I heard her calling me, I think she must have died that night. She felt so close.

RENEE   Do you hate the person?

MAGGIE   There's a line in the Bible, something about, whoever hurts a child, better he should have a millstone around his neck and be cast into a pond or something. I guess I think that about him. Can you imagine, living with that, having done that, all your life? You'd be better off dead.

RENEE   What if it's a woman?

MAGGIE   A woman? No, it couldn't be a woman.

RENEE   Why not? Why not. Women are equal to men, aren't they?

MAGGIE   No, a woman couldn't hurt a child like that.

RENEE   I thought you were the big women's libber.

MAGGIE   No, it wouldn't be a woman. A woman would feel what it was like. She would feel...empathy. No. No woman would do that to a child. To another woman.

> RENEE *gives a small laugh. Doorbell rings.*

(*hesitates*) Want me to get that?

RENEE   Okay.

> MAGGIE *goes out to the door. Door opens. Murmur of male voices.*

MAGGIE	(*re-enters*) It's the mounties.
RENEE	What do they say?
MAGGIE	They want to talk to you. Oh Jesus, the kids!
RENEE	(*gets up slowly, stands there*) *You* see what they want.

> MAGGIE *goes back into hall. Murmur of her voice and male voice.*

MAGGIE	Mrs. Gifford asked me to take a message.
RCMP	Well, we've been out to the workshop, it was open, but there's no one inside.
MAGGIE	The workshop? Are the kids in the workshop?
RCMP	No, it was Mr. Gifford she was worried about, I understand.
MAGGIE	Mr. Gifford?
RCMP	Mrs. Gifford put in a call to us about half an hour ago, but we've checked and there's no one in the shop. The lights are on but there's no one around. Actually, maybe she should lock up, it's Halloween and the kids get up to things on Halloween.
MAGGIE	(*comes back into kitchen*) They say there's nobody in the shop.
RENEE	I phoned the police. I told them I thought he was going to kill himself in the shop.
MAGGIE	What? My god, what? Renee.
RENEE	That's what I told them. What are they doing

now?

MAGGIE   They've gone.

RENEE   Gone! They can't go. Tell them to go back!
(*gets up, grabs* MAGGIE) Go on, tell them to
go back!

MAGGIE   But he's not there!

RENEE   (*runs out into hall*) He's there!

          Door opens. —Shuts.

       (comes back) They've gone. They drove away.
(*starts to rock herself back and forth*) I want you
to know...I loved him...I loved him. (*reaches for
the telephone, dials*) Yes, this is Mrs. Gifford
again. Yes, I called you before. Your men have
just left. They were here and they just left. Get
them back. No, stop them, and get them back.
No, my husband's there. He's there. No, there's
a trap door in the workshop. There's a room,
under the shop. Yes, there's a sort of air raid
shelter under the shop. He's got another room
down below. —It's a plywood slab painted blue.
There are jugs of stuff on top of it. They're
glued. They stay on the slab when you pull it
up. It's a secret room. It's on the house
description. Yes. Yes. —Thank you. Yes, I'll
hold. (*does not turn*)

          MAGGIE *is staring at her. Puts down her
          drink. Gets up slowly. Turns and looks out
          toward us, through the sliding doors.*

       Yes, yes? John Gifford. Yes. Yes. Yes, that
one. Mrs. Benton lives next door. Yes. —Yes,
yes, it's a secret bunker or something. A
plywood slab, painted blue. There're jugs of

stuff, turpentine or something, on top, but they're glued down, so when you pull up the slab they don't fall off.

MAGGIE   (*turns and looks at* RENEE) I hope you live a long time, Renee. I hope you have a long long life.

RENEE   Forgive me.

MAGGIE   Never.

She turns and goes to the sliding doors, slides them open, and runs out into the night toward the workshop.

RENEE   Yes. Yes, I'll hold on.

Dim spot on RENEE's *face, hold briefly, then go to black.*

The End.